teaching reading with the other language arts

Edited by

Ulrich H. Hardt
Portland State University

For the IRA Committee on Reading and Its Relationship to the Other Language Arts

INTERNATIONAL READING ASSOCIATION
800 Barksdale Road Newark, Delaware 19711

INTERNATIONAL READING ASSOCIATION

Library of Congress Cataloging in Publication Data
Main entry under title:

Teaching reading with other language arts.

Includes bibliographies.
1. Reading—Addresses, essays, lectures. 2. Language arts—Addresses, essays, lectures. I. Hardt, Ulrich H., 1936- II. IRA Committee on Reading and Its Relationship to the Other Language Arts.
LB1050.T38 1983 372.4'1 82-25525
ISBN 0-87207-734-9

Contents

IRA Reading and Its Relationship to the Other Language Arts Committee, 1978-1982

Phylliss J. Adams
University of Denver

Richard Ammon
Pennsylvania State University

Margaret A. Atwell
California State College

Mark W. Aulls, *Chair* 1981-1982
McGill University

Morton Botel
University of Pennsylvania

Norma Dick
Clovis, California,
Unified School District

Annette R. Guenther
Lake Havasu City, Arizona

Ulrich H. Hardt, *Chair* 1980-1981
Portland State University

Jack Howell
Clearwater, Florida

Judith W. Irwin
Purdue University

Angela M. Jaggar
New York University

Margaret E. Joyce
Charlottetown, Prince Edward Island

Heath Lowry
University of the Pacific

Dorothy Menosky
Jersey City State College

Arlene M. Pillar
Fordham University

Lynn K. Rhodes
University of Colorado

Sandra A. Rietz
Eastern Montana College

Nancy W. Seminoff
Northern Michigan University

Nancy Shanklin
Bloomington, Indiana

Iris M. Tiedt, *Chair* 1978-1980
San Jose, California

Dorothy J. Watson
University of Missouri at Columbia

LaVisa Wilson
Auburn University

Rosemary Winkeljohann
St. Ursula Villa Elementary School
Cincinnati, Ohio

Foreword

Researchers and theorists in the field of language have long agreed that reading and the other language arts are inextricably related. Despite this tacit authoritative agreement, the integrated language arts approach rarely manifests itself in practice. Publishers and children's text authors continue to produce one series of materials for reading, one for grammar and usage, one for spelling, one for writing, one for phonics, one for comprehension, ad infinitum, ad nauseum. Similarly, teachers and administrators routinely schedule separate periods of time for reading and language arts. Colleges of education perpetuate the dichotomy by offering sets of courses in reading and sets of courses in language arts, each taught by different faculties who are often in different departments.

Thus, it is gratifying to see a volume like this one which not only provides discussion of the theoretical foundation for the integration of the language arts but also provides practical suggestions for K-12 educators as well as teacher trainees. Working over several years, Ulrich Hardt offers these discussions which were written by professional leaders in the field of reading. Practical ideas are included for organizing an integrated language arts curriculum at elementary, middle school, and secondary levels. Certainly, this volume will be an invaluable resource for any teacher who believes in the intrinsic relationship of the languag arts and desires to implement that integration in the classroom.

Jack Cassidy, *President*
International Reading Association, 1982-1983

About This Book...

Teaching Reading with the Other Language Arts, edited by Ulrich Hardt, discusses the intrinsic relationship of the language arts and provides practical ideas for organizing an integrated curriculum at elementary, middle school, and secondary levels.

This International Reading Association volume was sent to all IRA Comprehensive Members on record at the time copies came off the press. Interested readers may order copies from IRA, Department AA, PO Box 8139, 800 Barksdale Road, Newark, Delaware 19714, USA.

Individual Members US$7 Others US$10

Ask also for a free copy of IRA's Publications Catalog which describes all currently available titles, including other volumes concerned with reading and the language arts.

Preface

The seeds for this volume were sown by the International Reading Association with the appointment in 1978 of the Reading and Its Relationship to the Other Language Arts Committee. The first committee presented a Preconvention Institute at the 1979 IRA Convention in Atlanta on the narrower topic of "teaching reading holistically." Some of the papers were originally prepared for that occasion, but they have undergone extensive revisions as the committee changed and continued to talk and work together, and as a new emphasis arose which is now reflected in the thrust of this monograph.

As the project developed and our thinking deepened, the hope of producing a holistic method of teaching reading and the language arts shifted and discussion focused on the integrated teaching of the language arts.

One thing that has not changed is the audience addressed by the publication—classroom teachers, language arts theorists, and curriculum developers and directors—in short, the people who most likely can effect a change in the teaching of the language arts in our schools. This book is offered to them with the hope that the theoretical discussions and practical ideas will be immediately useful.

As with any book written collaboratively, one can expect to find a variety of styles and a spread of opinions. The collaborators believed from the beginning that total agreement was impossible as well as unnecessary. For that reason, the contributors present their own definitions of critical terms as they introduce them. Differences and divergencies also are singled out and commented upon in the final article dealing with problems and issues.

Finally, it should be pointed out that this book need not necessarily be read from the front to the back; it is arranged under the subdivisions of Foundation and Theory, Teacher Training, Classroom Practices, and Summary and Issues. Readers are directed to the sections and articles of most interest to them.

UHH

Part One
Foundation and Theory

Relating Reading and Other Language Arts: A Need for Reasoned Decisions

Mark W. Aulls
McGill University

Tasha, a sensitive 8 year old, holds a native love for all creatures. She has reached the last page of *Black Beauty*, and the tears are streaming down her face. In murmurs to herself, she affirms the depth of her special caring. And now this caring overwhelms her, and she sobs. New feelings about life have grown within her while reading and vicariously living this story.

For three days following the conclusion of *Black Beauty*, Tasha read her favorite parts to two close girl friends in her neighborhood. Together they shared their reactions to each part. At bedtime for two nights, Tasha reread these same parts to her cats, Fluffy and Browny. On the third day she drew a picture of herself and Black Beauty in a splendid field dimpled with her favorite flowers. Perhaps this was a kind of final monument to *Black Beauty* and the feelings and shared experiences surrounding her reading. Tasha's voluntary reading is often deeply meaningful for her. Home activities such as speaking, listening, art, and writing quite naturally flow from meaningful reading experiences.

What happens so naturally outside formal schooling should be no less likely to occur weekly during the course of formal schooling. Yet the extent to which children do relate reading and language in the classroom depends on whether teachers, writers of instructional programs, or designers of curriculum deliberately plan to provide regular opportunities for children to engage in relating reading and other language activities. One purpose of this article is to review theoretical and instructional alternatives relevant to planning how to integrate reading and other forms of language learning in elementary and secondary classrooms. The second purpose is to engage teachers and planners in the process of reexamining the relationship between reading and language arts instruction. The apparent decline of public trust in teachers and the general posture of the back to basics movement clearly signal that educators are expected to be able to provide more than intuitive biases to support their actions in teaching reading and language skills. They are expected to be able, upon demand, to provide deliberate and well reasoned explanations for their instructional actions.

Models of the Reading and Language Process

Pearson and Kamil (1980) have suggested that nothing could be more practical for teachers to possess than a model or theory of the reading process. While at face value many teachers might not agree with this admonition, models do provide deeper insights into the nature of reading and language, thereby opening new instructional perspectives. Often such insights enable a teacher to formulate a deliberately reasoned philosophy for: 1) selecting instructional goals and methods, 2) assessing individual students' reading and language problems, and 3) planning the uses of teacher and pupil time in the classroom.

All teachers hold biases toward instruction, and these biases guide their instructional actions as well as what they require students to do in the classroom. However, some teachers are controlled by implicit and unreasoned biases. As long as biases are not deliberately reasoned, teachers cannot account for what children can be expected to learn from instruction. Theoretical models of reading and language offer a deliberately reasoned framework through which educators can reflect upon the potential interfaces between reading and language and can derive expectations and principles for how to relate reading, speaking, writing, and listening instruction. Clearly, the gaps between theoretical models that describe reading and language processes and the goals or principles of reading and language instruction cannot be too discrepant. If they are, then either our theories or our practices must be changed to account for what and how children learn. Thus, what is true in theory must be true in practice and vice versa.

What follows is a description of four of the most influential models used to explain reading and language processes in the past decade. The term *model* usually refers to carefully reasoned metaphors (Pearson & Kamil, 1980), logical representations and visual or physical images (Brodbeck, 1959; Lachman, 1960; Turner, 1965). Models attempt to explain the essence of complex processes, to generate research, and to aid theory building. Models do not claim to be direct representations of reality. Unlike theory, a model's truth or falsity is not directly testable. The models to be reviewed are the skills model, the processing model, the discourse model, and the comprehension model. The social linguistic model will not be considered here since it is fully discussed in the Crafton paper elsewhere in this volume.

Skills Model

The skills model draws many of its assumptions about learning from the psychology of behaviorism (Skinner, 1957) and is in harmony with the philosophy of logical atomism (Russell, 1967). Reading is viewed to be a complex unitary skill which must be learned through direct instruction in contrast to natural acquisition. The most global skills of reading are word identification and comprehension. Association and stimulus response learning are primarily used to explain subskills learning. Subskills learning is assumed to depend heavily upon breaking down each subskill into atomistic units of content to which simple responses or classes of responses are accurately and automatically associated. The subskills content is derived primarily by an analysis of the linguistic units in text to be decoded and understood. This analysis usually relies upon the findings of structural linguistics. Most proficient subskill learning is believed to occur when subskills are ordered from simple to complex and when each stimulus (linguistic units within each subskill) is ordered into stages of presentation which then cause stages of responses to each stimulus (Samuels & Schachter, 1978).

While the reader's knowledge of language is recognized as an integral part of reading print, reading is not considered to be a natural language process that can be learned without instruction. Learning to read is viewed to be much like complex motor skill learning. This learning distinction sets the skills model apart from other models of reading. An emphasis on reading as a meaning-centered process and on early and frequent exposure to text is not viewed to play a central role in the initial phases of learning to read. Skinner's application (1957) of operant conditioning to verbal behavior (text and speech) has not been accepted as an adequate account of early language acquisition nor have related behavioristic theories such as mediational S-R learning (Clark & Clark, 1978; Pavio & Begg, 1981). However, behaviorism is still the primary learning theory relied upon by skills models to explain reading acquisition or lack of it.

Although behaviorism has not disappeared, its dominance has been replaced in the field of psychology by various branches of cognitive psychology. In the 1960s, the approach to language taken by structural linguistics was replaced by transformational grammar. Nonetheless, the skills model still seems to be pervasively relied upon as the basis for the planning and implementation of reading and language arts instruction. The most primitive component of this legacy appears to be educators' belief that reading and language should be logically analyzed into units of linguistic knowledge which, in turn, must be learned through instruction. Linguistic knowledge is taught by having learners make associations between classes of stimuli and classes of responses, and through practice. Common types of reading and language instructional principles which grow out of a skills model follow:

1. It is necessary for sound instruction to decompose language and text into a series of subskills which are

defined as specific content with one or more specific correct or incorrect responses.
2. All reading and language subskills must be directly observable and testable in order to assess whether they have been learned.
3. By logical task analysis, subskills can be ordered into a learning sequence which all students must pass through in order to progress successfully from the acquisition of lower to higher order skills.
4. Accuracy and automaticity of responses to spoken language units represent evidence of the extent to which a subskill has been learned, as well as readiness to progress to a more complex subskill.
5. Subskills learning gradually leads to higher levels of performance on the complex unitary skills of reading, listening, and speaking.
6. Meaning acquisition is the terminal outcome of reading and listening.
7. The expression of meaning is the terminal outcome of having learned writing and speaking.

Psycholinguistic Processing Models

Psycholinguistics is one branch of cognitive psychology which is primarily concerned with the mental structures and operations that make everyday communication possible (Foss & Hakes, 1978). Communication via language has been the principle area of interest of psycholinguistics. Rather than viewing human language and thought as understandable in terms of stimulus and response chains, their relationship is studied with the view that human beings are like a relatively complex information processing system (Glucksberg & Danks, 1975). Three primary questions have led to a variety of psycholinguistic processing models for language and reading: 1) What does one know when one knows language? 2) How does one use language knowledge when producing or comprehending speech or text? 3) How does one acquire knowledge about language and use it in processing spoken or written language? Chomsky's theory of language knowledge as it applies to linguistic competence (Chomsky, 1965) and to grammar and its underlying phonological system (Chomsky & Halle, 1968) and syntactic systems (Chomsky, 1965, 1968, 1972, 1976) has been central to the development of psycholinguistic models of speech and text processing. More recent models have relied on case or text grammars which focus on conceptual-semantic relations within or between sentences.

In the most general sense, psycholinguistically based processing models focus on describing what processes involved in speaking and reading explain production and comprehension. One major psycholinguistic model for speech processing is called the analysis-by-synthesis model. It is succinctly described by Neisser (1967) as an activity where "one makes a hypothesis about the original message, applies rules to determine what the input would be like if the hypothesis were true, and checks to see whether the input is really like that" (p. 194). The analysis-by-synthesis (or hypotheses test) model of language appears to explain best how young children acquire language knowledge (Clark & Clark, 1978). This model of speech processing was followed by a variety of processing models of reading (Goodman, 1967, 1974, 1976, 1980; Gough, 1972; Rumelhart, 1977; Smith, 1971; Stenovitch, 1981).

The models differ in their explanations of how the reader links knowledge of language and information on the printed page to get meaning. And there is literature to explain how these models differ. Currently, interactive processing models seem to be viewed as the most plausible for explaining proficient reading. The latest revisions of Goodman's models (1974, 1980) and Rumelhart's original model (1977) are interactive processing models. Each model views reading as a highly interactive process where linguistic units in the text—from the semantic, syntactic, lexical morphemic, morphophonemic to the graph-phoneme level—are used as needed by the reader to construct meaning during the cumulative processing of sentences in a text. Thus readers rely heavily on their prior knowledge of language to initiate the reading of text. In addition, Goodman (1980) emphasizes the importance of the tentativeness (in contrast to confidence) of the reader and the deliberate acquisition of reading strategies such as sampling, self-correcting, and confirming meaning. Finally, metalinguistic awareness of how language works and the ability to treat language as an object appear to facilitate efficient strategy acquisition, such as self-correcting mistakes (Lesly, 1980) and monitoring or confirming meaning relationships during text processing (Gleitman, 1972; Waterhouse, Fischer, & Ryan, 1980).

In short, the psycholinguistic processing models reject the concept that the reading process is a global unitary skill made up of an assembly of subskills. Furthermore, they emphasize that reading is a process that builds on available language competence. In all processing models, the reader must be very active (as opposed to passive) during reading. In each model, knowledge of language helps the reader progress directly or indirectly from print to meaning through the use of language cues in the text. The efficient and effective reader integrates the available cues and uses the full cue redundancy in the text to facilitate fluent meaning-prediction and sampling. Finally, most of these models imply that the reader acquires processing strategies for how to map language knowledge onto text by reading meaningful text and by extensive opportunities to simultaneously hear and follow along visually as a text is read orally.

At least five principles of instruction follow from psycholinguistic processing models of reading and language.

1. Language, whether oral or written, is a highly interdependent system which *should not* be fractionated into atomistic units for all aspects of instruction. When this is done, its redundant and cohesive properties, which signal meaning, are destroyed.
2. Language and text become meaningful during processing, and the active use and coordination of varied levels of meaning representations are necessary at any stage of acquisition. Hence, there are more reasons to argue against the decomposed and sequenced presentation of

language and text subskill units than to argue against the presentation of a meaningful text unit which is highly predictable on the basis of what the pupil already knows about grammar.

3. Young children will find it easiest to read or write language which is natural to them as speakers and listeners and is derived from their own prior experiences. Thus, they will be motivated by their own intrinsic needs to explore their world through reading and writing.
4. Knowledge and awareness of relationships between language and print are not sufficient to produce or comprehend efficiently written text. It is also necessary for children to learn strategies for predicting, organizing, reflecting upon, and monitoring what is read, written, or spoken.
5. Young children learning to read or write their native language are competent oral language users. This competence constitutes a primary resource for learning that reading is constructing meaning and writing is producing a meaningful message. As children grow older, they are increasingly more capable of consciously self-regulating their language knowledge and deliberately using it to judge, manipulate, or coordinate its structures and meanings during reading, writing, speaking, and listening.

Discourse Models and Comprehension Models of Reading

Discourse models of language and comprehension models of reading maintain the emphasis of psycholinguistic models on the importance of language knowledge to the production of speech and comprehension of written text. However, discourse and comprehension models emphasize the extreme importance of replacing sentence grammars with text grammars and recognize the function of pragmatics in understanding both (Morgan & Green, 1980; Morgan & Sellner, 1980). Discourse models of language are derived primarily from literary theory, rhetoric, stylistics (Brewer, 1980), tagmemics (Pike, 1967), and text grammars (Grimes, 1975; Van Dijk, 1972, 1973). Models of reading comprehension are derived from cognitive psychology and the fields of memory, inferential reasoning, schema theory, and text grammars.

Moffett (1968) offers a simple definition of *discourse*: a piece of verbalization complete for its original purpose. *Text* is a form of discourse. Text is referred to by Halliday and Hasan (1976) as a passage of whatever length that forms a unified whole. It must have cohesion in the sense that any interpretation of some element in the discourse is dependent on that of another and it cannot be successfully decoded without this property. Text must also have coherence in the sense that it is ordered into networks of meaning relationships or coherent properties. Native speakers are able to process, produce, receive, and interpret text or discourse as unified meaningful relationships, not merely as a sequence of sentences (Grimes, 1968; Halliday & Hasan, 1976; Van Dijk, 1973).

Moffett offers a discourse model of language and language learning and suggests that the relationship among speaker-listener-subject is the ultimate context within which language and reading growth can be matched to the mental operations of the learner (Moffett, 1968; Moffett & Wagner, 1976). Variations in learning occur as functions of full participation in the sender-message-receiver relationships and practice in abstracting and relating understandings derived from text or speech which enable understanding to occur. Morgan and Sellner (1980) tend to support these observations. They argue that the balance between what the reader (listener) superimposes upon text and infers from it enables understanding to occur. Some outcomes of learning language and reading are to abstract the common structures of a variety of discourses, to classify them in memory, and to use them in ways that assist the comprehension of spoken and written discourse as well as the production of meaning as speech or text.

Models of reading comprehension are concerned with explaining how readers understand and remember text. Some of the more important dimensions of the reading comprehension process which have evolved from comprehension models are:

1. The reader's active use of prior knowledge (schemata or frames) before, during, or after reading to assist understanding;
2. The varied functions of inferencing in organized meaning during and following reading;
3. The importance of the reader's knowledge of text structures in constructing or reconstructing text meaning during or following reading; and
4. The influence various text properties have on the reader's understanding and recall of information from different kinds of text.

Comprehension models enable us to explain conditions prior to, during, and following reading which influence the reader's understanding or recall of text information as opposed to just those conditions operating during reading.

The most direct relationship between discourse or text models and comprehension models lies in describing the knowledge of discourse common to speech and text on the one hand and the child's uses, organization, and transfer of this knowledge during reading, discussions, writing, and drama on the other hand. By merging concepts from the discourse and comprehension models, it becomes possible to generate useful questions about the possible learning and developmental relationships to be expected between reading and other language processes. For example, what types of relationships exist among the acquisition and control of discourse knowledge and composition strategies and the acquisition and control of text knowledge and processing strategies displayed during reading (Aulls, 1981)?

By merging theoretical constructs which are compatible and common among models of discourse and reading comprehension, the following principles for relating reading and language instruction seem plausible:

1. There cannot be too great a gap between what a reader, listener, speaker, or writer already knows and the topic read, heard, discussed, or written about.

2. Prior knowledge of the world and of language influence how the reader/listener interprets the author's intended message as well as how the speaker/writer produces a message.
3. Growth in understanding the potential interrelationships among reading, speaking, listening, and writing depends upon the opportunity for the learner to participate in each process and play different roles (author, reader, listener) when the processes are combined for different purposes. Hence, artificially dichotomizing reading and other language arts into separate subjects totally ignores the transfer learning benefits derived by interfacing similar tasks such as learning about the function of topical relationships when reading text, writing text, or planning a speech.
4. Inferencing strategies used to respond to a text are not necessarily different from those used to rewrite one's own drafts of composition. The same principle applies to speaking and listening contexts such as debates, panels, or discussions. Furthermore, the most reasonable means of assessing whether specific inference strategies are under the control of a learner is to observe whether they can be used spontaneously in more than one situation, such as reading and writing; speaking and writing; speaking, writing, and listening; or reading, writing, and listening.
5. When reading, writing, or listening, the learner must know how and when to generate inferences between prior knowledge and the literal discourse information. The use of questions to guide such inferences is equally applicable in each situation.
6. During instruction using methods like the language experience approach, young children will benefit from reading their own language written down. They also benefit from being read to and hearing and following along with the reading of children's books (Holdaway, 1979). In the latter case, this is the means for them to learn what structures define different types of discourse

and how to expect the meaning of adventure stories, fables, and folktales, to be organized. In turn, this knowledge enables them actively to predict and remember different types of discourse as readers or listeners. At later stages of cognitive growth, the range and types of discourse forms they choose to express themselves when writing are influenced.

7. Children throughout formal schooling daily need to read, write, and react to a variety of discourse forms or genres. At the present time, narrative and descriptive materials dominate elementary schooling. This is in direct contrast to secondary education where exposition tends to be the most frequently assigned reading and writing genre. It is perhaps not surprising that at the time a considerable gap appears to exist between students' abilities to understand and write expository prose in contrast to narrative materials.

For elementary and secondary educators who are concerned about what outcomes to expect from attempting to relate reading and language instruction, these models provide a rich array of information and research from which to derive instructional principles. The models themselves allow educators to gain deeper insights into the nature of language processes and the reading process; they do not have any necessary bearing on how and what teachers actually teach as reading and language arts. However, models do describe what appears to be necessary for children to learn and what is possible for them to learn as producers and comprehenders of language and text. In this sense, theoretical models, and the instructional principles generated from them, enable educators to assess the gap between typical current teaching practices and what appears to be necessary and/or possible for children to learn.

Effective Classroom Instruction

It is important to recognize that the predominant elementary and secondary practices for teaching reading and language reflect the tenets of the skills model. Since the 1970s, the linguistic and psychological assumptions of the skills model have been considered by many scholars to be limited in explaining reading and language learning. Thus, a considerable gap exists between the dominant instructional practices and the more recent theoretical explanations of reading and language. The reasons for this gap may be due to: 1) the knowledge base simply expanding much more rapidly than educators have been able to absorb it into classroom practices; 2) colleges and universities not being as successful as in the past in disseminating the newer theoretical ideas so that they are translated into programs and methods of instruction; 3) the limited availability of published reading series reflecting the post-1960 models of teaching the language arts and reading; or 4) the realities of teacher effectiveness in implementing classroom instruction somehow precluding many teachers from using instructional principles derivable from post-1960 models of reading and language. Since teachers have greater control over their own classroom than over curriculum and program development, the fourth reason is most plausible and relevant and will be discussed further.

The instructional principles which theoretical models can be used to generate are of little consequence if teachers do not find ways to use them in the classroom. A large number of elementary and secondary classroom observational studies have been carried out and reported since the early 1970s. Clear and significant differences have been found among teachers whose classroom actions in selecting and planning learning activities and engaging pupils in learning tasks, classroom management, and direct teaching of small groups have a strong and positive influence on reading and language achievement (Brophy, 1980; Duffy, 1980; Durkin, 1978-1979; Good, 1980; Stallings, 1980).

Equally significant effects on pupil performance and attitudes have been reported for the manner in which pupil/pupil time is used independent of the teacher for cooperative small group learning (Johnson, 1981), peer tutoring (Allen, Feldman, & Devin-Sheehan, 1979), the involvement of pupils in learning centers (Kosmoski & Vockell, 1978), or structured pupil/pupil activities (Devries & Slavin, 1978).

Teachers who do not provide opportunities for most students to learn do not engage pupils' attention and keep them on task during reading and language instruction (Rosenshine & Berliner, 1979). Teachers who are effective can minimize the inefficient use of teacher/pupil and pupil/pupil directed learning time, prevent misbehavior, obtain student cooperation and responsibility for learning, and obtain high pupil involvement in assigned work specifically. Furthermore, those teachers who spend far less time in teacher-directed small group instruction than whole-class or individual instruction do not have as great an impact on student learning (Stallings, 1980). Finally, teachers who provide the psychological opportunity to learn are those who: 1) offer more rather than less structure, 2) set high goals and figure out how to realistically enable students to obtain them, 3) know how to select and assign students to learning tasks in which they can succeed, 4) believe students can and do learn, 5) develop an effective reward structure for the majority of pupils in a class, and 6) give more time for discussion and review in small group instruction as well as timely feedback to individual students.

At face value, there appears to be no reason to believe that the effective teacher could not select and implement principles of reading and language instruction derived from any of the theoretical models discussed. Only lack of relevant knowledge about recent models of language and reading would appear to preclude an efficient teacher from using the instructional principles derived from newer process models, to integrate reading and language instruction. However, Duffy (1980) has pointed out that there may be two types of efficient classroom teachers who are successful in teaching reading. One type is an excellent technician. This type of teacher actively engages students in reading tasks and keeps them on task. This is done by selection of activities to fit available time constraints and enable smooth activity flow. The only instructional problem is that, by pursuing any activity, this type of teacher gives little consideration to what students actually learn.

The second type of efficient teacher is a decision maker. This type of teacher does everything the technician does (or at least achieves the same effect) but reflectively makes instructional decisions during the day-to-day flow of classroom management. This teacher focuses on planning, assessing, and revising instruction to promote learning rather than focusing solely on student involvement. Thus, this teacher appears to be the most inclined toward, and most capable of, using and implementing the instructional principles derived from any of the more recent models of reading and language.

For teachers who are already relatively effective in the classroom there are several important instructional implications which arise from newer instructional principles for language and reading.

1. Teaching knowledge should not be confused with teaching strategies.
2. Teaching both strategies and knowledge is necessary to foster growth in reading, writing, speaking, and listening.
3. The gap between the knowledge or strategies a student can spontaneously use and those to be taught should not be too great or they will not be learned.
4. The ultimate learning goal for reading and language should be the acquisition of knowledge and strategies which the student can deliberately self-regulate. This achievement appears to be necessary for knowledge or strategies to be successfully transferred to new reading, speaking, listening and/or writing contexts (Ryan, 1981).

Knowledge of language or text refers to word concepts; redundant cues in oral or printed discourse that signal meaning relationships; anaphora; rules for identifying critical text properties such as the distinction between superordinate and subordinate topics or main ideas; and text or discourse structures such as dialogue and monologue, description versus explanation, argument versus comment, cause/effect versus time sequence patterns, blank versus rhymed verse, the narrator's functions in a story, event chains in a story, and kinds of questions and their expected response requirements. In contrast to knowledge, *strategies* refer to action-oriented steps for arriving at a particular outcome (Ryan, 1981). In the case of reading, the following strategies are used: 1) prediction, 2) backward inferences, 3) self-correction of mistakes, 4) confirmation of predictions, 5) steps for monitoring meaning construction or reconstruction, 6) steps for using prior knowledge to fill in meaning gaps arising during reading and to elaborate on the author's intentions or concepts, and 7) the uses of self-generated questions to organize the author's intended meanings.

In writing, examples of strategies are 1) activating sufficient prior knowledge before writing to have something meaningful to say, and 2) during rewriting, using questions such as "Did I say everything I need to say?" "Did I transmit feelings?" "Did I elaborate sufficiently on my major ideas to allow most readers to understand their value?" and "Are my ideas sufficiently organized to be understood by my intended audiences?" Such questions will guide and monitor future drafts (Graves, 1980; Schiff, 1978). Finally, strategies for revising and/or editing what has been written must include self-regulated routines for checking spellings, cohesion of statements, and coherence of the overall message components (Berieter & Scardamalia, 1980). Once students can learn strategies or knowledge at the level where they can be activated correctly when cued by the teacher, students are ready to practice and apply them in pairs or cooperative small groups without further instruction by the teacher, except for feedback and discussions when needed.

While stimulus/response instructional methods can be used to teach some types of reading and writing knowledge, they are not effective in teaching word meaning concepts, problem solving rules or principles, strategies, and most forms of text structure. Furthermore, teaching new strategies entails modeling as opposed to didactic or discovery methods of teaching knowledge (Aulls, 1980). *Modeling* refers to instruction where the teacher shows students how to activate and use strategic steps. For example, by using a cloze exercise, the teacher can model predictions, confirm predictions, and self-monitor through oral and/or visual demonstration (Aulls, 1980). Guided questions can be modeled to teach more active inferencing (Goodman & Burke, 1980; Pearson, Hansen, & Gordon, 1979). Another example of teaching reading comprehension strategies is explaining how to use self-generated questions during reading (Andre & Anderson, 1978-1979) or how to use a question guide when revising drafts during writing (Bereiter & Scardamalia, 1980). In both situations, reconstruction of the writer's intended meaning is facilitated.

Conclusions

There now exists a variety of reasonably valid alternative models for explaining the production and comprehension of language and text. These models can be very useful in generating instructional principles for relating and integrating reading and language instruction in the elementary and secondary classroom. At the present time, it appears to be very clear that a skills model offers only a partial explanation of language and reading processes. One of the most important limitations is in explaining how subskills knowledge become integrated into the unitary global skill of proficient reading and writing. On what grounds should we expect principles of instruction generated from the skills model to be more dominantly used than those from other models to teach reading and language arts? The major instructional principles generated from a skills model tend to separate and fragment reading and language instruction with little regard to the language and cognitive resources available to children at different stages of development. Furthermore, they may give teachers the impression that their primary function is only to teach the skills activities in published programs, rather than to take responsibility for direct instruction of any skills and strategies (Duffy, 1980; Durkin, 1978-1979).

Effective teaching does place realistic constraints on what instructional principles teachers are likely to choose and to implement in the classroom. However, effective teachers are free to choose from newer instructional principles which are quite different from those afforded by a skills model. Will effective teachers be willing to explore and employ new alternative principles for reading and language instruction? If they are not, will it be possible for them to establish new teaching roles and to establish new conditions for what and how pupils learn? How teachers answer these questions and ask whether we follow the suggestions about teacher training Rietz makes later in this volume will largely determine whether any changes occur in how children are taught reading and language in the next decade. More importantly, the answers may determine the opportunities children have to become literate, for the answers may also determine what literacy means to our society.

References

Allen, L.V., Feldman, R.S., & Devin-Sheehan, L. Student success and tutor verbal and nonverbal behavior. *Journal of Educational Research*, 1979, *72*, 142-149.

Andre, M.A., & Anderson, T.H. The development and evaluation of self-questioning study technique. *Reading Research Quarterly*, 1978-1979, *14*, 607-623.

Aulls, M.W. *Developmental and remedial reading in the middle grades*. Boston: Allyn and Bacon, 1978.

Aulls, M.W. The nature and function of context during reading and writing. In V. Froese & S. Straw (Eds.), *Research in language arts: Language and schooling*. Baltimore, Maryland: University Park Press, 1980.

Bereiter, C., & Scardamalia, M. From conversation to composition: The role of instruction in a developmental process. In R. Glaser (Ed.), *Advances in instructional psychology*, 2. Hillsdale, New Jersey: Erlbaum, 1980.

Brewer, W.F. Literary theory, rhetoric, and stylistics: Implications for psychology. In R.J. Spiro, B.C. Bruce, & W.F. Brewer (Eds.), *Theoretical issues in reading comprehension*. Hillsdale, New Jersey: Erlbaum, 1980.

Brodbeck, M. Models, meaning, and theories. In L. Gross (Ed.), *Symposium on sociological theory*. Evanston, Illinois: Row, Peterson, 1959.

Brophy, J. Advances in teacher research. *Journal of Classroom Interaction*, 1980, *15*, 1-7.

Chomsky, N. Review of B.F. Skinner's *Verbal behavior*. *Language*, 1959, *35*, 26-58.

Chomsky, N. *Aspects of the theory of syntax*. Cambridge, Massachusetts: MIT Press, 1965.

Chomsky, N. *Studies on semantics in generative grammar*. The Hague: Mouton, 1972.

Chomsky, N. Conditions on rules of grammar. *Linguistic Analysis*, 1976, *2*, 303-351.

Chomsky, N., & Halle, M. *The sound pattern of English*. New York: Harper & Row, 1968.

Clark, H.H., & Clark, E.V. *Psychology and language: An introduction to psycholinguistics*. New York: Harcourt Brace Jovanovich, 1977.

De Beaugrande, R. Design criteria for process models for reading. *Reading Research Quarterly*, 1980-1981, *16*, 261-315.

Devin-Sheehan, L., Feldman, R., & Allen, L.V. Research on children tutoring children: A critical review. *Review of Educational Research*, 1976, *46*, 355-385.

Devries, D., & Slavin, R. Team-games-tournaments: A research review. *Journal of Research and Development in Education*, 1978, *12*, 28-35.

Duffy, G.G. Teacher effectiveness research implications for the reading profession. Unpublished paper presented at the California Reading Association Conference, San Diego, California, December 1980.
Durkin, D. What classroom observations reveal about reading comprehension instruction. *Reading Research Quarterly*, 1978-1979, *14*, 481-533.
Foss, D.J., & Hakes, D.T. *Psycholinguistics: An introduction to the psychology of language.* Englewood Cliffs, New Jersey: Prentice-Hall, 1978.
Glucksberg, S., & Danks, J.H. *Experimental psycholinguistics.* Hillsdale, New Jersey: Erlbaum, 1975.
Good, T. Research in teaching. Unpublished paper delivered at the American Educational Research Association Conference, Boston, April 1980.
Goodman, K.S. Reading: A psycholinguistic guessing game. *Journal of the Reading Specialist*, 1967, *4*, 126-135.
Goodman, K. The reading process. Unpublished paper presented at the Western Learning Symposium, Bellingham, Washington, 1974.
Goodman, K.S. The know-more and the know-nothing movements in reading: A personal response. *Language Arts*, 1979, *56*, 657-663.
Goodman, Y.M., & Burke, C. *Reading strategies: Focus on comprehension.* New York: Holt, Rinehart and Winston, 1980.
Goodman, K.S., & Goodman, Y.M. Learning about psycholinguistic processes by analyzing oral reading. *Harvard Educational Review*, 1977, *47*, 317-333.
Gough, P. One second of reading. In J. Kavanaugh & I. Mattingly (Eds.), *Language by ear and by eye.* Cambridge, Massachusetts: MIT Press, 1972.
Graves, D.H. An examination of the writing process of seven year old children. *Research in the Teaching of English*, 1975, *9*, 227-241.
Graves, D.H. A new look at writing research. Unpublished paper, Writing Process Laboratory, University of New Hampshire at Durham, 1980.
Grimes, J. *The thread of discourse.* The Hague: Mouton, 1975.
Halliday, M., & Hasan, R. *Cohesion in English.* London: Longman, 1976.
Holdaway, D. *The foundations of literacy.* Sydney, Australia: Ashton Scholastic, 1979.
Johnson, D. Student-student interaction: The neglected variable in education. *Educational Researcher*, 1981, *10*, 5-10.
Kosmoski, G.J., & Vockell, E.L. The learning center: Stimulus to cognitive and affective growth. *The Elementary School Journal*, 1978, *79*, 47-54.
Lachman, R. The model in theory construction. *Psychological Review*, 1960, *67*, 113-129.
Liberman, I.Y., Shankweiler, D., Fowler, C., & Fischer, E.W. Phonetic segmentation and recoding in the beginning reader. In A.S. Reber & D.L. Scarborough (Eds.), *Toward a psychology of reading.* Hillsdale, New Jersey: Erlbaum, 1977.
Moffett, J. *Teaching the universe of discourse.* Boston: Houghton Mifflin, 1968.
Moffett, J., & Wagner, B.J. *Student centered language arts and reading, K-13.* Boston: Houghton Mifflin, 1976.
Morgan, J.L., & Green, G.M. Pragmatics and reading comprehension. In R.J. Spiro, B.C. Bruce, & W.F. Brewer (Eds.), *Theoretical issues in reading comprehension.* Hillsdale, New Jersey: Erlbaum, 1980.
Morgan, J.L., & Sellner, M.B. Discourse and linguistic theory. In R.J. Spiro, B.C. Bruce, & W.F. Brewer (Eds.), *Theoretical issues in reading comprehension.* Hillsdale, New Jersey: Erlbaum, 1980.
Neisser, U. *Cognitive psychology.* New York: Appleton, 1967.
Pavio, H., & Begg, I. *Psychology of language.* Englewood Cliffs, New Jersey: Prentice-Hall, 1981.
Pearson, P.D., Hansen, J., & Gordon, C. *The effect of background knowledge on young children's comprehension of explicit and implicit information.* (ED 169 521)
Pearson, P.D., & Kamil, M.L. *Basic processes and instructional practices in teaching reading.* (ED 165 118)

Pike, K. *Language in relation to a unified theory of the structure of human behavior.* The Hague: Mouton, 1967.
Rosenshine, B., & Berliner, D. Academic engaged time. *British Journal of Teacher Education,* 1979, 3-16.
Rubin, A. A theoretical taxonomy of the differences between oral and written language. In R.J. Spiro, B.C. Bruce, & W.F. Brewer (Eds.), *Theoretical issues in reading comprehension.* Hillsdale, New Jersey: Erlbaum, 1980.
Rumelhart, D. Toward an interactive model of reading. In S. Dormic (Ed.), *Attention and performance,* 6. Hillsdale, New Jersey: Erlbaum, 1977.
Russell, B. *The problems of philosophy.* London: Oxford University Press, 1967.
Ryan, E. Identifying and remediating failures in reading comprehension: Toward an instructional approach for poor readers. In T.G. Waller & G.E. Mackinnon (Eds.), *Reading research: Advanced in theory and practice* (Vol. 2). New York: Academic Press, 1981.
Samuels, S.J., & Schachter, S. Controversial issues in beginning reading instruction: Meaning versus subskills emphasis. In S. Pflaum-Conner (Ed.), *Aspects of reading education.* Berkeley, California: McCutchan Publishing, 1978.
Schiff, P.M. Problem solving and the composition model: Reorganization, manipulation, analysis. *Research in the Teaching of English,* 1978, *12,* 203-210.
Skinner, B.F. *Verbal behavior.* New York: Appleton-Century-Crofts, 1957.
Smith, F. *Understanding reading.* New York: Holt, Rinehart & Winston, 1971.
Stallings, J. Allocated academic learning time revisited, or beyond time on task. *Educational Research,* 1980, *9,* 11-16.
Stenovich, K.E. Toward an interactive compensatory model of individual differences in the development of reading fluency. *Reading Research Quarterly,* 1980-1981, *16,* 32-65.
Turner, M.B. *Philosophy and the science of behavior.* New York: Appleton-Century-Crofts, 1965.
Van Dijk, T. *Some aspects of text grammars.* The Hague: Mouton, 1972.
Van Dijk, T. Text grammar and text logic. In J. Petofi & H. Rieser (Eds.), *Studies in text grammar.* Dordrecht, The Netherlands: D. Reidel, 1973.
Waterhouse, L.H., Fischer, K.M., & Ryan, E.B. *Language awareness and reading.* Newark, Delaware: International Reading Association, 1980.

Reading, Writing, Speaking, Listening: Language in Response to Context

Margaret A. Atwell
California State College at San Bernardino

At Lincoln Elementary School, a well trained and competent fourth grade teacher is going about her daily routine, including the teaching of reading and language lessons.[1] At this moment the children in the classroom are beginning their reading lessons by writing, talking, listening, and reading. Observing the scene we see several children scattered around the room, writing in journals, part of their daily routine. These children may choose to keep their writing to themselves, private records of private thoughts, or they may—and quite often do—deposit their journals in the class's *To Read* box, knowing that the next day each child will find a written response from the teacher. Occasionally, these written conversations lead to oral dialogues between the original two communicators. Sometimes other participants will join the exchange, either orally or in writing through their own journal entries. It is also not uncommon for dialogues to grow into full class discussions. Often, the written correspondence engenders no oral response, but remains a personal exchange between two readers/writers.

One boy sits at a table that holds an array of books, pamphlets, charts, and notes. He has gathered these texts as sources to be used for a science experiment he is planning. Since he hopes to involve other class members in the project, he is listing directions for his classmates' use. At the moment, he is copying directly from one text that he has found to be more useful than his other sources, but he is simplifying or expanding the directions.

Two boys who are inseparable friends sit near each other, each reading a book authored by the other. This transaction is a culmination of several days of activity. Earlier, each had decided that he wanted to write a story, a pragmatic decision that led to several linguistic choices: Each boy thought up the story he wanted to tell, a process that involved a lot of talking, laughing, and sharing as they decided on their messages. Each had also drawn illustrations for the books that helped clarify both the text and the ideas they were composing. When each boy felt that his story had reached a presentable form, he carefully prepared the final manuscript. Using materials provided in the classroom, the boys helped each other bind their books. After they finish reading, they will add their books to a growing library of books written, illustrated, and bound by other classmates/authors. As they read a friend's writing, they often giggle, poke each other as a means of giving attention to a particular part of the text, or sometimes groan at a silly joke. To some teachers, this deportment might indicate a lack of seriousness toward learning. The teacher in this classroom understands that these boys are comprehending and appreciating text and, in their most natural way, they understand that language is a transactional and social event.

During the morning, the teacher will read aloud a story selected by members of the classroom's "textbook adoption committee." All members of the class are eligible to be part of this committee and, because it is a sought-after position, membership is rotated. The members of any particular committee will nominate books to be considered for selection and ultimately for shared oral reading. As on any committee of its sort, personal and political issues arise: Some members favor one author's work and will lobby in favor of a book by that writer. Other choices reflect issues of individual interest, and books reflecting those topics are considered. Genre enters into the selection procedure as well: Various members like science fiction, humor, fantasy. Members name certain books they hope are selected. Through negotiation, members ultimately do choose a book for their teacher to read aloud.

Occasionally, while reading the selected book, the teacher will pause before turning a page and ask the children to predict what they believe might happen next. The teacher will read on and, perhaps, stop again to briefly discuss whether students' predictions had been correct. Children will sometimes display a sensitivity to the author's craft by modeling stories of their own after a particular text, its genre, structure, or topic.

This class is not, however, without its failures. For a while, considerable effort had gone into a classroom newspaper. Children wrote stories, edited, and laid out the tabloid that would eventually be typed and copied so that each member could have a copy. This project didn't last long, however, because the teacher felt that the publishing activity was too dependent upon her. (The teacher was the only class member with access to the mimeograph machine.) Instead, the teacher turned over to an editor and staff a large bulletin board where announcements, stories, news, and features could be posted.

Although the principal praises the teacher for doing a marvelous job of integrating the language arts, the teacher denies doing anything of the sort. To the teacher, integration implies a bringing together of elements that would otherwise not unite. This teacher understands language another way: Language is always whole, is always social, and exists only because communicators need a medium through which to connect. The teacher in this classroom knows that readers are also speakers, listeners, and writers, and that to be any one of these means you will be all of them. To become any of these, language always must be used as an active process of sharing meaning.

Language and Language Instruction

All teachers hold beliefs about the nature of language that affect the instruction and settings they provide in their classrooms (Burke, 1980; Harste & Burke, 1980). Teachers with altering models will teach quite differently (Barr, 1974-1975; DeLawter, 1970; Mitchell, 1978). Whether they are consciously aware of their model, teachers are remarkably consistent in their classrooms as they operationalize theory into daily lessons (DeFord, 1981), and their model affects the verbal interactions that go on in their rooms (Feathers, 1980; Siegel, 1980). There is some evidence that teachers who clarify their models modify their classroom practice (DeFord, 1979; Marine, 1981; Stansell & Robeck, 1979). The importance of teachers' developing theory of language cannot be understated. That is why this volume, concerned with the teaching of reading, has begun by discussing such theories. As Aulls points out in the first chapter, there is a gap between our latest knowledge concerning the nature of language and its application in classrooms. This article began by describing one teacher's application of personal belief that language is a sociopsycholinguistic process. The remainder of this chapter will take a more direct look at the model behind the teacher's method.

Language as a Holistic Process

The teacher in this article believes language is a social process that occurs when communicators acting within real contexts send and receive messages, a process that involves the mental process of linguistic information. The teacher's model is one that reflects a sociopsycholinguistic orientation that assumes

- There is a single language process that expresses itself in alternate forms but that acts as a shared core for each of its expressive modes.
- Reading is one expression of language that is intricately affected by and, in turn, affects other linguistic expressions.
- What is learned through one expression is used to support language growth and expression in each other mode.

Language, in this model, is the relational base for the language arts of reading, writing, speaking and listening. Each linguistic expression is but an orchestration of the interactive symbolic, syntactic, and semantic information operative within any particular context. The distinct expressions of reading, writing, speaking, and listening exist as a result of the manner in which the language base relates to the contextual setting and the pragmatic choices made by the language user, not because each possesses intrinsically discrete sets of subskills.

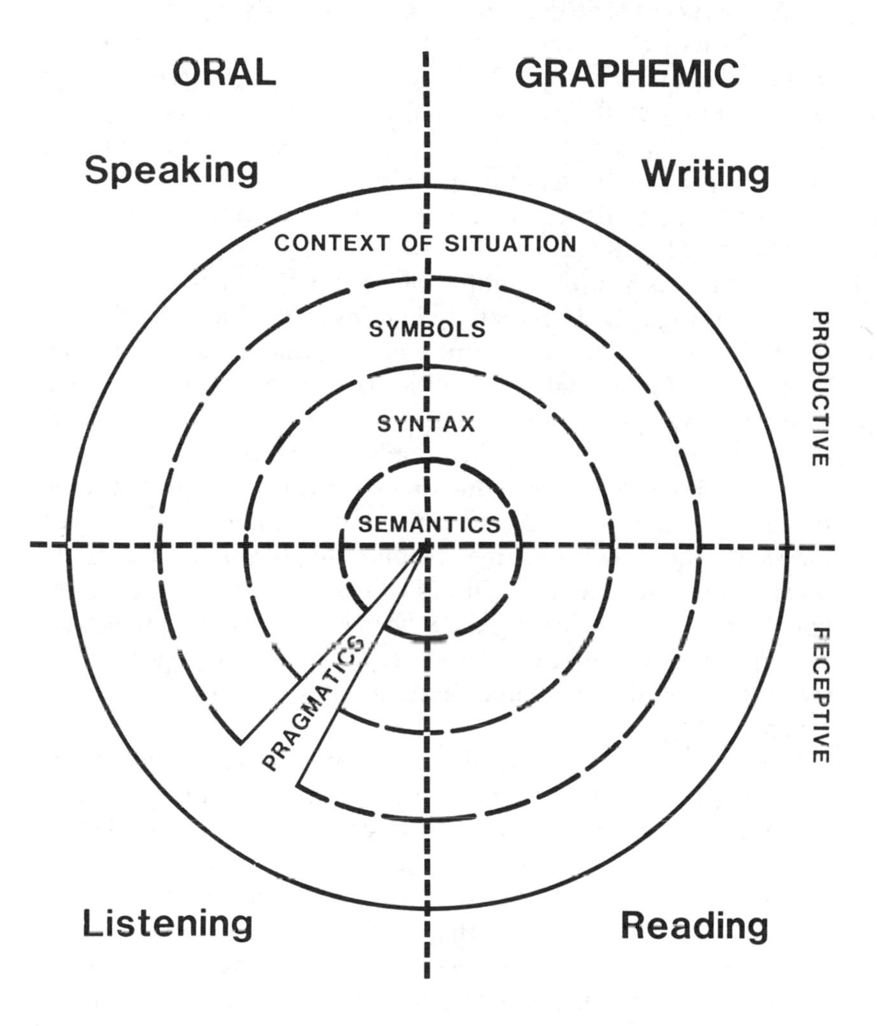

Figure 1. Language as the representational format responding to situational context.

For example, language responds to its setting in either oral or written form. In its oral representation, the symbol system emerges as phonemes; the syntax may range from formal to casual, depending upon the setting and intent and supported by paralinguistic features, and the semantic system will eliminate those references that time and proximity can support.

In its written forms, the symbols will be graphemic, the syntax may range in formality and will incorporate punctuation as a visual counterpart of paralinguistic information. The semantic system may require inclusion of referential information that will provide a meaningful scaffold for the message being received by an audience outside the communicator's own spatial and temporal setting.

This description might imply that language is static, but it never is. Language is an activity and involves either receptive or productive use. When the setting demands that a message be sent, language will be produced as either writing or speech. In either case, language producers will determine a message; select from the semantic, syntactic, and symbolic fields available; and assemble those linguistic elements that, together, represent their thoughts. When the setting demands that language users receive a message, they will become readers or listeners. Receptive language requires language users to engage actively in meaning construction by anticipating the other's intent; making predictions concerning the message; and confirming, adjusting, and incorporating the evolving message into an existing mental scheme.

Pragmatics refers to the emersion of text in context and involves choices concerning the message, medium, and audience. The inital pragmatic choice in any communication is whether individuals will become participants. If the language users decide not to engage, that will be the end of it. If, however, language users decide to participate, they make a number of pragmatic decisions that will cut across and affect linguistic choices. Language users will first indicate they are entering into a communication contract (Tierney & LaZansky, 1980) and will begin to negotiate the terms of this agreement. At times this will seem direct. At other times, language users may make adjustments to the contract by evolving stances that affect field, mode, or tenor that other communicants did not expect (Harste, 1980). Communicators will also make pragmatic decisions concerning the medium that will convey the message. For instance, at times language users' pragmatic decisions will lead them to decide that the best medium for the message is a formal letter. At other times, they may decide that a casual telephone call is the best conveyance.

The relationship between text and context is always interactive. Seldom, if ever, does one language expression exist in isolation. Typically, language users switch from one mode to another in linguistic encounter. In every conversational setting, communicators will be speakers at one moment and become listeners the next.

Although it might be tempting to cite the monologue as an example of a language expression that exists in isolation, we must immediately consider that, in order to produce speech, language users will monitor utterances and become their own inescapable audience. Vygotsky (1962) has suggested that the dynamic counterroles of speakers-listeners enable young children to use inner speech as a guide for both their thinking and their actions and eventually lead to mature thought and language.

Language in its graphemic forms allows the same flexibility. Authors can proceed fluently through the process of producing text but, at some point, this movement may stop as the writers become the readers of the text. They may do this in order to generate more text, to reformulate a part of the message, reword, check for consistency, or simply to hear the discourse. When the purpose has been met, the reader once again writes (Atwell, 1980). Although it is seldom discussed this way, reading is as recursive as writing. It is quite natural for readers to pause, reread, or scan ahead or back and then continue reading the text.

In point of fact, all language is recursive. Whether the movement is backward into text, forward in mind, or across contexts into alternate modes, language is never static. The movement between linguistic forms and functions is so natural that language users are seldom aware of the interfacing they do. It seems unlikely that so easy an interaction would demand that a communicator draw upon completely distinct sets of competencies as the skills orientation describes the nature of language arts. Rather, the fluidity suggests that, in natural settings, language users move from dealing with psycholinguistic information in one way to orchestrating that same information into another expression, as demanded and supported by context and social need. While there are features which have become conventions unique to each individual language expression, each is comprised of the same elements. The representational format of language—that is to say, whether it occurs as reading, writing, speaking, or listening—is no more or no less than the user's response to the situational context of that language.

Theory and Practice

Language curriculum must be a macrocosm of the language model it serves. Our classroom practice should never violate what we know about the process in our teaching of that process. Language, as it occurs in natural settings, does not build itself from the bottom up in componential pieces. Instead, it comes as whole messages directed through appropriate media at audiences who have some need to receive that message.

Instruction in language has, for too long, focused on linguistic competence as a goal and the mastery of the rules and skills of language as the means of its achievement. Teachers who cordon off the school day into time zones belonging to instruction in reading skills, or writing skills, or speech, or listening practice fail to represent to their students language as it is used in any other setting but this one. Teachers who integrate the language arts as a means of reinforcing skills development, or who add writing, speech, or listening to reading classes as a means of language enrichment, are working in rhetorically impoverished settings (Daigon, 1980) that suggest little of the true dynamics of language. Cazden and Hymes (1972) suggest that teaching should foster "communicative competence," the knowledge that allows children to decide on the appropriate uses of language in settings that demand communication for real social purposes. Children must be allowed to talk with one another, read, listen, and write, not because they need to strengthen their language skills, but because, as social beings, they need to communicate.

Note

[1]While the teacher and classroom described herein are fictitious, very real people and places like those described do exist. Refer to Milz (1980), Canady (1980), and Weurtenberg (1980).

References

Atwell, Margaret. The evolution of text: The interrelationship of reading and writing in the composing process. Unpublished doctoral dissertation, Indiana University, 1980.

Barr, Rebecca. The effect of instruction on pupil strategies. *Reading Research Quarterly*, 1974-1975, *4*, 555-582.

Burke, Carolyn. Comprehension centered reading curriculum. In Beverly Farr & Darryl Strickler (Eds.), *Reading comprehension resource guide*. Bloomington, Indiana: Indiana University Printing, 1980.

Burke, Carolyn. Reading is. . .the process and the learner. Presentation at Twelfth Annual Reading Conference, Kean College, October 1975.

Canady, R.T. Psycholinguistics in a real-life classroom. *Reading Teacher*, 1980, *34*, 156-159.

Cazden, Courtney, & Hymes, Dell. (Eds.), *Function of language in the classroom*. New York: Teachers College Press, 1972.

Daigon, Arthur. Rhetorically-based and rhetorically-deficient tasks: An explanation. In Judith Meagher & William Page (Eds.), *Language centered reading instruction*. Storrs: Reading Language Arts Center, University of Connecticut, 1980.

DeFord, Diane. Teachers' models of reading: The effect of instruction in a higher education program. Presentation at the NRC Annual Meeting, San Antonio, 1979.

DeFord, Diane. Children's growing concepts of story: Their impact on reading and writing. Presentation at the Southwest Regional IRA Conference, San Antonio, 1981.

DeLawter, Jaynce. Oral reading errors of second grade children exposed to two different reading approaches. Unpublished doctoral dissertation, Columbia University, 1970.

Feathers, Karen. Comprehending as the extended creation of text. Presentation at the NRC Annual Meeting, San Diego, 1980.

Goodman, Yetta, & Burke, Carolyn. Reading: Language and psycholinguistic bases. In Pose Lamb & R. Arnold (Eds.), *Reading: Foundations and instructional strategies*. Belmont, California: Wadsworth, 1976.

Harste, Jerome. Language as social event. Presentation at AERA Annual Meeting, Boston, 1980.

Harste, Jerome. Reading comprehension: The instructional connection. In Beverly Farr & Darryl Strickler (Eds.), *Reading comprehension resource guide*. Bloomington, Indiana: Indiana University Printing, 1980.

Harste, Jerome, & Milz, Vera. The teacher variable: An interview with Vera Milz. In Beverly Farr & Darryl Strickler (Eds.), *Reading comprehension resource guide*. Bloomington, Indiana: Indiana University Printing, 1980.

Marine, Lynn. Influences of inservice language instruction on classroom verbal interaction. Presentation at IRA Annual Conference, New Orleans, 1981.

Milz, Vera. The comprehension centered classroom: Setting it up and making it work. In Beverly Farr & Darryl Strickler (Eds.), *Reading comprehension resource guide*. Bloomington, Indiana: Indiana University Press, 1980.
Mitchell, Katherine. Patterns of teacher-student responses to oral reading errors as related to teachers' previous training in different theoretical frameworks. Unpublished doctoral dissertation, New York University, 1978.
Siegel, Marjorie. Discourse processing from the perspective of speech act theory. Presentation at the NRC Annual Meeting, San Diego, 1980.
Stansell, John, & Robeck, Carol. The development of theoretical orientation to reading. Presentation at the NRC Annual Meeting, San Antonio, 1979.
Tierney, Robert, & LaZansky, Jill. The rights and responsibilities of readers and writers: A contractual agreement. *Language Arts*, 1980, *57*, 606-613.
Vygotsky, L.S. *Language and thought*. Cambridge, Massachusetts: MIT Press, 1962. (originally published in 1934)
Weurtenberg, Jacque. Reading for writing/writing for reading. In Darryl Strickler (Ed.), *The affective dimension of reading resource guide*. Bloomington, Indiana: Indiana University Printing, 1980.

Oral and Written Language: Related Processes of a Sociopsycholinguistic Nature

Linda K. Crafton
Northeastern Illinois University

For many, the term *language learning* calls to mind a young child developing the oral mode necessary to communicate with the initiated members of the language group. However, the terms *language* and *language learning* imply all the communicative power one accrues as one grows in a literate society—the whole of one's communicative competence. That competence not only takes the form of oral language but written language as well. Indeed, it is through the four expressions of the generalized language process—reading, writing, speaking, listening—that one becomes a fully functioning, contributing member of the Human Club. In Halliday's terms, language learning in all of its expressions is a "learning how to mean process" (1975).

These four aspects of language have three language systems in common: graphophonemic (phonemic), syntactic, semantic. These rule-bound systems are actively (and tacitly) discovered by young children who actually hypothesize linguistic rules and evaluate those guesses as they compare their attempts to the adult system. Through contact with the people around them, and by listening to oral language that refers directly to objects and events, children begin to attach language to reality (Soderbergh, 1975). Sociolinguists state that in addition to the child's acquisition of structural rules of the language, another set of rules which refers to the appropriate time to speak, the appropriate time to remain silent, and the linguistic code used when speaking must be learned (Hymes, 1967; Williams & Naremore, 1969).

Children do not need to be taught language (Cazden, 1969); they need the appropriate experiences which demonstrate obvious contrasts. Concomitantly, children deduce linguistic rules, test them, obtain feedback, modify or revise them, and try them out again in yet another context. That oral language learning is indeed a hypothesis-testing enterprise seems to be widely accepted by psycholinguists; however, such a thesis is only a tentative postulation when the question is one of literacy. It is the intent of this paper to explore some basic tenets of oral language acquisition and their relationship to reading and writing development. The theoretical perspective adopted here is of a sociopsycholinguistic nature. Sociopsycholinguistics suggests the importance of studying cognitive and linguistic processing in light of the context, environmental and linguistic, in which it occurs.

A Functional View of Language

Written and oral language are functional. If they were not, Goodman (1979) contends, there would be no reason for their development and presence in societies. Goodman suggests that literacy, reading and writing, is learned in the same way as oral language. He further states that if language learning is, as Halliday has said, learning how to mean, then literacy learning is learning how to mean with written language. Though written language is comprehended in much the same way as oral language, its use to communicate over time and space appears to serve as an explanation for the extended development of written language as compared to oral language.

Recent research (Y. Goodman, 1976; Harste, Burke, & Woodward, 1979) documents the hypothesis that children who grow up in a literate society begin to develop literacy long before they experience a formal classroom setting. Children learn very early (as young as two and three years) that print represents meaning. They learn general and specific meanings in varying situational contexts: road signs, fast food restaurants, toothpaste cartoons, tissue boxes. For example, in Harste, Burke and Woodward's study, when preschoolers were shown U.S. Mail printed on the side of a mailbox, they gave the following responses:

"A birdie flew." (Nathan, age 3)
"American Picture Sign." (Allison, age 4)
"Put in Mail." (Jonathan, age 5)
"U.S. Mail." (Emily, age 6)

Children seem to learn the form of language through its functional use. All expressions of early language development may be interpreted as the child's progressive mastery of a "functional potential" (Halliday, 1975). If reading and writing development are seen as natural extensions of oral language development in the context of developing functions, then it follows that fulfillment of that functional potential is accomplished through continuous and natural experience in using the language expressions. A functional view of language learning posits that all language learning, oral and written, should be easy and pleasurable because it is naturally acquired.

Learning to Speak, Read, and Write Is Natural

Most children develop oral language easily and naturally. They do so in the noisy environment of their family in which they daily interact with others in a myriad of situations. Children who are strongly motivated to understand and be understood, move rapidly toward the dialect of their family and their immediate society community. The rapidity with which children develop oral language has given rise to varying views of that development. Some linguists view the process of acquiring language as an innate process which unfolds maturationally; others view it as an increasingly complex linkage of responses. In contrast to both of these views is a posture that sees language as a personal and social invention (Goodman & Goodman, 1976; Halliday, 1975; Harste, Burke, & Woodward, 1979). This view of language development, both oral and written, focuses on the communicative need as a prime motivator for language acquisition. Such a view of language development falls in line with Halliday's belief of function preceding form, and it puts the emphasis on that creative aspect of language which enables society to cope with novel situations and ideas.

The latter account of language development is the position taken in this paper. Just as children hear speech before they can produce it, children growing up in a literate society encounter written language before they have a need to communicate in that expression. Children encounter environmental print at every turn: they go to McDonald's for lunch, they accompany Mom and Dad to Safeway for groceries, they go to K-Mart for toys, and on their way to all of these places they encounter *Stop* signs, *No Parking* signs, and other familiar print. Children encounter books and are read to; they color and scribble and try to write their names, and through all of these processes and encounters they become aware of written language and its uses—an awareness that leads as naturally to interaction with print as with any other part of their environment. It is probable that many children are reading, writing, and inventing their own spelling rules (Read, 1975) long before their parents are aware of the children's written language growth (Goodman & Goodman, 1976).

Children utilize the technique of testing hypotheses as oral and written language develop. During oral language development children establish cognitive and linguistic categories (Brown & Bellugi, 1964). Based on experience, they allocate an object, event, or distinctive feature to a particular category. To learn to distinguish cats from dogs, for example, children must be in a situation where the differences between the two matters and the distinctive features can be established. When children are learning to use a specific grammatical rule, they must experience the rule applied in varying situational contexts in which the rule makes a difference. Based on the feedback received as different linguistic hypotheses are tested, the notion of object, event, or configuration will be modified to fit the category or a new one will be established.

This hypothesis testing is used constantly to construct various states of comprehension in all areas of a child's life; it is employed in oral language acquisitions and is used when the child begins to encounter print as well. Because children already know some language and know that language cannot exist apart from meaning, they quickly understand that the semantic core penetrates all print (and speech). Children also use what is already known to learn that syntax has a specific structure which forms predictable patterns and that graphemes, like phonemes, have distinctive features which form categories.

As children grow, the knowledge base expands, and they must learn to make the most economical use of the linguistic contextual cues received, for it would be time consuming and energy wasting to go through every category or hypothesis tried each time there was a need to identify an event or sequence (Baghban, 1979). There is a basic predictability about most things in life, and language is no exception. In language, predictability exists because of graphophonemic, syntactic, and semantic repetitions. Experience helps children take note of these repetitions and consistencies so that the redundancy can be used at different levels to eliminate nonsignificant alternatives (Smith, 1971). In fact, it is experience that allows each of us to make predictions in both speech and reading. For example, how many times have you guessed what the exact word is going to be at the end of a phrase or sentence when engaged in dialogue or reading a book? Small children become familiar with and enjoy predicting words, phrases, sentences, and even entire story structures in texts with repetitive or cumulative sequences. It is this ability to predict based on experience which allows us to use few acoustic and visual cues, to know what we can safely ignore in conversation or written language without a meaning loss. As children discover the predictability of language in all of its expressions, the global, pervasive hypothesis testing strategy is used to learn to speak, read, and write quite naturally.

The Difference between Oral and Written Language

Halliday states (1969, pp. 26-37) that what is common to every use of language is that it is meaningful, contextualized and, in the broadest sense, social. Several decades ago modern linguistics shifted its emphasis from written to oral language. In so doing, written language came to be seen as something other than language. Clearly, written language can perform the functions of language, hence, it must be language (Goodman & Goodman, 1976). In an examination of the differences between oral and written language, Goodman and Goodman (1976, p. 7) present the following chart so that one may easily consider the basic characteristics of the alternate language forms.

	Oral	*Written*
Input/output medium	Ear/voice	Eye/hand
Symbolic units	Sounds and sound patterns	Print and print patterns
Display	Over time	Over space
Permanence	Instantly perishable, unless electronically recorded	As permanent as desired
Distance limits	Distance between encoder and decoder limited, unless amplified or electronically transmitted	Distance between encoder and decoder unlimited
Structure	Phonological surface representation of deep structure and meaning	Orthographic surface representation of deep structure and meaning

Goodman and Goodman point out that speech is best suited for present, face-to-face encounters, whereas writing lends itself to communication over time and space. Probably the cultural reason for written language development was this need to extend communications between people separated by time and distance.

Even in a highly literate society such as our own, oral language is usually the first language form developed by most individuals. However, overwhelming evidence of oral language primacy may not necessarily mean that meaningful interaction with print is delayed until the child has demonstrated some control of speech. Currently, there is empirical evidence being amassed (Y. Goodman, 1976; Harste, Burke, & Woodward,

1979, 1980) that shows that very young children not only have some awareness of form and function of written language but also make some use of their developing literacy long before their control of oral language is fully functional (Goodman & Goodman, 1976).

Halliday (1975) states that children know what language is because they know what language does, how it functions in their world. Halliday has presented a view of children's models of language in terms of the functions which Goodman and Goodman have applied to written language.

Halliday's Functions of Language

Instrumental: I want
Regulatory: Do as I tell you
Interactional: Me and you
Personal: Here I come
Heuristic: Tell me why
Imaginative: Let's pretend
Informative: I've got something to tell you

Halliday suggests that these functions appear approximately in the stated order, and he stresses the fact that function precedes form in language development. Goodman and Goodman share some examples of children's awareness of the functions of language through their observations of young children. Any mother or father who takes a child grocery shopping is keenly aware of how well established is the "I want" (Instructional) function of language. As the parent and child move through the aisles of the grocery store, the child quickly eyes the cereal or candy seen on TV and begins to demonstrate just how well this function of language is understood by echoing the commercials: "I want Apple Bran Cereal for breakfast."

Children as young as 2 years are aware of the regulatory function of language. Show any young child a STOP sign, and you are likely not only to get a response as to what the sign says but also a comment about exactly what you are supposed to do when you are in a car and come upon that sign.

Letter writing is one example of the interactional function of language. I began writing letters to my niece when she was 3 years old. She enjoyed receiving them and always wanted to respond to what I had written. Her early letters were written in a prerepresentational form of language that often looked like scribbling; however, there was always an underlying message base which she dictated to her mother after she had judged her graphic display to be satisfactory. As she grew older, her letters began to look more letter-like; for example, she began her letters with "Dear Aunt Nin" and closed with "Love, Amie," and her orthography moved toward the standard form. She also began to show evidence of an awareness of the situational difference in oral and written language; because interacting through print is not situationally supported, the written language must express aspects of messages which are supported by other means during oral language conversations.

The personal function of written language may actually come earlier than some of the other functions. One way the personal function is established in speech early in children's lives is the constant effort made by parents to get their children to say their own names. Likewise, the first words in written language that children are interested in representing are their own names. Goodman and Goodman suggest that this written representation of self becomes a way of establishing oneself in a literate environment.

Goodman and Goodman state that "...the last three [functions], heuristic, imaginative, and informative, are the functions for which written language is most heavily used in literate societies" (1976, p. 11). As the experiences and language of children expand, so do the functions the language serves. No matter to what use the language is put or what expression is being employed, what seems to be common to every use of language is that it is meaningful, contextualized, and social (Halliday, 1975).

Oral Language and Reading

Research related to the beginning phase of reading is in its infancy; similarly, we know little about reading and its relationship to speaking. Smith (1976, pp. 297-299) makes several points relating to the onset of reading:

The first is that children probably begin to read from the moment they become aware of print in any meaningful way, and the second is that the roots of reading are discernible whenever children strive to make sense of print before they are able to recognize many of the actual words.

Third, not only are the informal mechanics of reading unnecessary in these initial stages, they may well be a hindrance. It is the ability of children to make sense...that will enable them to make use of the mechanics....Fourth, words do not need to be in sentences to be meaningful, they just have to be in a meaningful context....

Learning to speak and learning to read are both meaning-based processes. As children organize, categorize, and generally make sense of their worlds, they become aware of print as different from other graphic information available to them. After that distinction is made, children begin to assign meaning to the print in the environment and thereafter expect it to be meaningful. Because interpreting and reacting to printed language may be a short step from interpreting and reaching to spoken units, oral language growth should be a primary concern when considering beginning reading (Artley, 1953).

Studies which have been concerned with the relationship between oral language and reading can be found in the literature; however, these studies have generally concerned themselves with children learning oral language in a natural setting but learning reading in a formal setting (Carroll, 1966; Samuels, 1978).

Children are naturally curious; this curiosity embraces not only a desire to learn but a wish to control. The child's urge to control even causes independent language practice as in the crib soliloquies Weir (1962) recorded from her 2 year old son. Likewise, given the proper instruments, children will play with written language. For example, they will create their own stories using wordless picture books, scribbling and drawing; and they will print spontaneously, differentiate pictorial information from graphic information, and learn the distinctive features used in writing on their own (Gibson & Levin, 1975). Read (1975) has even documented the orthographic inventiveness of young children. Given a child's curiosity, internal mechanisms, and experience with the world from birth, giving meaning to the printed page seems a natural and predictable behavior—one which should hardly surprise us or seem to be particularly difficult.

Building on the child's oral language strength is an important factor in learning to read and write. Ashton-Warner (1963) asks her students which words they would like to learn to read or write. She writes these very personal items on cards so that students may keep them to use whenever they like. The children typically use the lexical items to build stories which they can then read and share. Children learn to control the written environment very early and begin to recognize the relationships among speaking, reading, and writing.

Reading should be considered a natural event in a child's language development. Most home environments are naturally encouraging to a child's oral language growth; literacy development also should be treated naturally. That attitude toward reading, coupled with the interaction itself, seems to be the central characteristic for reading to occur. As noted previously, children respond very early to symbols in their environment. "When a child responds to a common symbol around the house, beginning reading should be considered to be occurring" (Ryan, 1977, p. 159).

Oral Language and Writing

Many parallels may be drawn between oral and written language. Theoretically, oral and written language development have been viewed similarly without challenge for a long period of time. Learning these processes from the part to the whole—that is, from single phonemic or graphemic units to larger and more complex linguistic structures—seemed as commonsensical as knowing when to come in out of the rain. Common sense no longer. Psycholinguists engaged in reading, writing, and oral language research are suggesting quite different views—ideas which recognize both the complexity and communicative nature of even the most rudimentary language functions.

Peters (1977), for example, suggests that speech development may have its genesis in a wholistic form, children attempting to produce whole phrases and sentences rather than single words. Similarly, current discourse models (Frederiksen,

1977; Kucer, 1980) suggest that writing proceeds in a gestalt fashion—moving from a global idea to its individual parts which must ultimately be presented on paper. Further, in support of a sociopsycholinguistic view of language development, Peters has found that the kind of language children produce varies as the context of situations varies. Likewise, writing behavior will vary as contexts vary (Busch, 1979; Harste, Burke, & Woodward, 1979). Current research in writing is just beginning to map the differences in writing performance and proficiency as situations change in and out of the classroom.

As spontaneously as children seem to learn to speak, the average child will scribble when given paper and pencil at 18 months, or earlier (Cattell, 1960). Clay's observations (1977) of infant classrooms lead her to the conclusion that when child discovery is valued and writing is encouraged, writing plays a significant role in early reading. Read uses his findings on inventive spellings (1975) to emphasize that young children naturally have a highly sophisticated intuitive understanding of phonology.

Baghban (1979) reports that her daughter, Giti, used oral language and writing as mutually reinforcing processes. Giti's parents used oral language to identify their written products to her which eventually led to her expectations that written language be as meaningful as oral language. At 24 months, Giti started to use relationships between sounds and letters to write. She began to use her oral language to elicit samples of drawing and writing from her parents—a procedure which helped to teach her the difference between the categories of drawing and writing. The identification of the partnership between oral language and written language firmly established the communicative nature of writing.

Children actively develop oral language in the supportive context of the family; similarly, they learn to process print in meaningful ways in terms of their worlds and what they know. Writing, too, can be viewed as a personal mode of learning, an extension of an individual's experience. Writing about ourselves and our experiences is one way of shaping and incorporating those experiences into the body of our past experiences. Harste,

Burke, and Woodward (1979) note that the "more fully representational uses of communication systems" by the children in their study was in the form of personal information; for example, writing their names. Writing as an act of revealing one's inner and outer worlds may begin with language close to the writer. Britton (1970) terms this language that tells us about the writer's expressive language; it is a form of writing that relies heavily on the situation in which it occurs for its interpretation. Britton believes this to be a principle of early writing and also the foundation on which all writing is built. As the writer develops, writing becomes more explicit; i.e., features previously omitted from expressive writing because they were implied are now included.

Children are active agents in constructing their own linguistic systems. As noted earlier, developing language is a process of generating and testing hypotheses. Nonthreatening language settings afford children the opportunity to play with the language, to experiment, to test hypotheses. Harste, Burke, and Woodward observed that many children in their study were more interested in hypothesis testing while engaged in the reading or writing process rather than demonstrating what they already knew about the language. Evidence of active hypothesis testing in writing has already been noted in the studies on invented spelling; Zutell (1978) suggests that young children's spelling errors provide evidence for the psychological reality of the use of the rule construction-hypothesis testing process in writing.

Revision in writing reveals a similar kind of exploratory-testing type of procedure (Graves, 1979). When children discover they have something to say, writing it down one time is usually not enough to make their meaning clear; a first draft may be only a testing of ideas and a testing of the structure through which to express those ideas. Reading what has been written may cause a reconsideration of content and lead to changing, cutting, revising—a process of discovering meaning through language as one thinks and plays on paper. Students can be observed trying out words or phrases or different structures to see how they fit the communicative intent of their message.

A Linguistic Data Pool

From their research on preschool reading and writing development, Harste, Burke, and Woodward cite the following language story.

> We showed Allison the word JELL-O, in mixed primary type and asked "What does that say?"
>
> Allison hesitated a moment, shrugged her shoulders, and then said, "I don't know, it should be a telephone number."

It appears that Allison had transformed the two l's into ones and the O into a zero. This language story is cited because it cogently demonstrates the cognitive flexibility of young children. Cook-Gumperz (1977) terms such flexibility "negotiability," a label which captures a child's willingness to use any available communication means in an attempt to make sense of the available input. Harste, Burke, and Woodward note that stories such as this one illustrate that at early stages of linguistic development, print information is not distinctively categorized from other information which they have acquired via alternative communication systems. The concept of negotiability is an important one as we come to understand that what the child knows about one expression of language can support growth and development in another expression of language. This conceptualization presupposes a parallel growth and development among the expressions of language. For example, what the child knows about how oral language operates becomes available data for the discovery and testing on how written language operates.

Burke (1978) suggests that each of us can be considered to possess a pool of language data, "constituted of a set of relations concerning how meaning is shared through language." Data for the pool may enter as any language expression—listening, speaking, reading, or writing experiences—and may exit as any one of the expressions. Evidence for this conceptualization is easily seen as we observe children "borrowing" story structure from an author they have heard or read for presentation of their own stories—an indication that that linguistic information (story schema) will be available for use in other settings as well.

Burke's conceptualization of a linguistic data pool clearly supports the notion that oral and written language growth are supportive, interrelated processes of a sociopsycholinguistic nature. It appears that what is known about oral language development has much to contribute to our understanding of early reading and writing development. The evidence which can be amassed as to their direct relationship in so brief a treatment as this underscores the theoretical notion of a common cognitive and linguistic base from which these processes expand and mature. A sociopsycholinguistic orientation to oral and written language development suggests important research avenues for initial print encounters in contexts which are increasingly valid ecologically—a corner of the inquiry pie long recognized by students of oral language development as indispensable to their pursuit. Instructionally, such a veiw calls into question the school environment which may be remiss in supporting the development of written language in natural contexts for the function and use of language outside the school.

Linguistic Data Pool

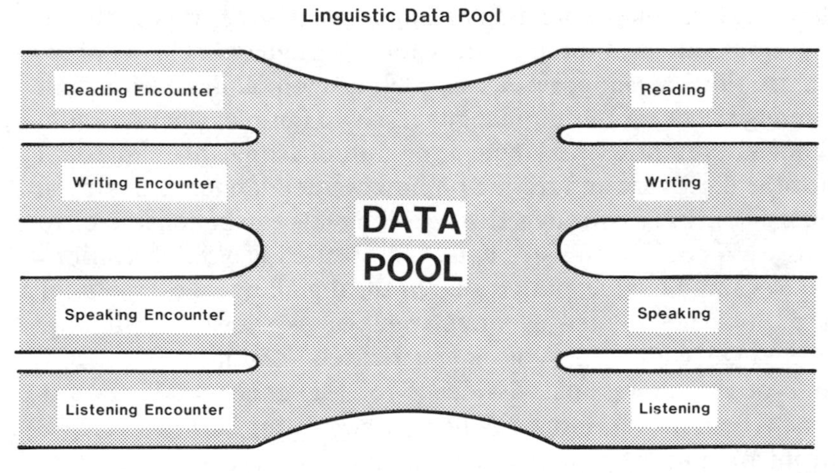

Harste, Burke, & Woodward 1979

References

Artley, A.S. Oral language growth and reading ability. *Elementary School Journal*, 1953, *53*, 321-328.

Ashton-Warner, S. *Teacher*. New York: Simon & Schuster, 1963.

Baghban, M. Language development and intial encounters with written language: A case study in preschool reading and writing. Unpublished doctoral dissertation, Indiana University, 1979.

Britton, J. *Language and learning*. Baltimore: Penguin Press, 1970.

Brown, R. *A first language: The early stages*. Cambridge, Massachusetts: Harvard University Press, 1973.

Brown, R., & Bellugi, U. Three processes in the child's acquisition of syntax. *Harvard Educational Review*, 1964, *34*, 133-151.

Burke, C.L. Reading as communication: Reading as language. Paper presented at the Annual Meeting of the National Council of Teachers of English, Kansas City, November 1978.

Busch, K. Unpublished masters research, Indiana University, 1979.

Carroll, J.P. Some neglected relationships in reading and language learning. *Elementary English*, 1966, *43*, 577-582.

Cattell, P. *The measurement of intelligence of infants and young children*. New York: Psychological Corporation, 1960.

Chomsky, N. *Aspects of the theory of syntax*. Cambridge, Massachusetts: MIT Press, 1965.

Clay. M. Exploring with a pencil. *Theory into Practice*, 1977, *16*, 334-341.

Clay, M. *What did I write?* London: Heinemann, 1975.

Cook-Gumperz, J. Socialecological perspectives for studying children's use of persuasive arguments. Paper presented at the Department of Sociology Seminar, Indiana University, November 1977.

Frederiksen, C. Processing units in understanding text. In R. Freedle (Ed.), *Discourse producation and comprehension*. Norwood, New Jersey: Ablex, 1977.

Gibson, E.J. The ontogeny of reading. *American Psychologist*, 1970, *25*.

Gibson, E.J., & Levin, H. *The psychology of reading*. Cambridge, Massachusetts: MIT Press, 1975.

Goodman, K. The know-more and the know-nothing movements in reading: A personal response. *Language Arts*, 1979, *56*, 657-663.

Goodman, K.S., & Goodman, Y.M. Learning to read is natural. Paper presented at a conference on theory and practice of beginning reading instruction, Pittsburgh, April 1976.

Goodman, Y. A study of the development of literacy in preschool children. NIE Research Grant Proposal, 1976.

Graves, D. Let children show us how to help them write. Unpublished manuscript, University of New Hampshire, 1979.

Halliday, M.A.K. Relevant models of language. *State of Language Educational Review*, 1969, *22*, 26-37.

Halliday, M.A.K. *Learning how to mean*. London: Edward Arnold Ltd., 1975.

Harste, J.C., Burke, C.L., & Woodward, V.A. Children's language and world: Initial encounters with print. In J. Langer & M.T. Smith-Burke (Eds.), *Reader meets author/Bridging the gap*. Newark, Delaware: International Reading Association, 1982.

Harste, J.C., Burke, C.L., & Woodward, V.A. Children's initial encounters with print. National Institute of Education grant proposal, 1979, 1980.

Hymes, D. The functions of speech. In John P. DeCecco (Ed.), *The psychology of language, thought, and instruction*. New York: Holt, Rinehart and Winston, 1967.

Kucer, S.B. A message based model of discourse production. *Occasional papers*. Bloomington: Indiana University, 1980.

Peters, A.M. Language learning strategies: Does the whole equal the sum of the parts? *Language*, 1977, *53*, 560-573.
Read, C. Children's categorization of speech sounds in English. Technical Report No. 197, Committee on Research. Urbana, Illinois: National Council of Teachers of English, 1975.
Ryan, J. Family patterns of reading problems: The family that reads together.... In Malcolm P. Douglass (Ed.), *All things considered*. Claremont, California: Claremont College, 1977.
Samuels, S.J. Controversial issues in beginning reading instruction: Meaning versus subskill emphasis. In Susanna Pflaum-Connor (Ed.), *Aspects of reading education*. Berkeley, California: McCutchan Publishing, 1978.
Smith, F. Learning to read by reading. *Language Arts*, 1976, *53*, 297-299, 322.
Smith, F. *Understanding reading*. New York: Holt, Rinehart and Winston, 1971.
Soderbergh, R. Review article: Language by ear and by eye. *Journal of Child Language*, 1975, *2*, 153-168.
Weir, R.H. *Language in the crib*. The Hague: Mouton, 1962.
Williams, F., & Naremore, R. On the functional analysis of social class differences in modes of speech. *Speech Monographs*, 1969, *36*, 77-102.
Zutell, J. Some psycholinguistic perspectives on children's spelling. *Language Arts*, 1978, *55*.

Part Two
Teacher Training

Training Teachers to Integrate the Language Arts: An Elementary Preservice Model

Sandra A. Rietz
Eastern Montana College

One of the primary responsibilities of the training program of language arts teachers is the development of teacher experiences which will minimize the discrepancies between what is known about learning processes/language and language processing/language acquisitions and development, and what is done in the public school classroom when language is "taught." Planning for, organizing, and building the program require an examination of basic considerations in language learning and classroom practices. Teaching the program requires teachers of teachers to organize for teaching and use many of the same methods they are advocating for use with children. Knitting together the gaps between theory/research and practice is a methodological problem as critical in the teacher training classroom as in the public school classroom.

Some Basic Considerations Prerequisite to Program Development

Language Acquisition

Though adults play an important role in the child's acquisition of language, the child directs the process. As Aulls' and Crafton's discussions in this volume show, adults do not teach children language nor do they teach children how to go about collecting, organizing, and using linguistic information.

Adults participate in children's language learning by providing the quantity of language in the environment necessary for children's language rule formations, the safety in which children can test newly formed rules, and the language interaction with the children required to verify and refine the shapes of language rules. That children do not approach linguistic information in a manner compatible with adults' sense of orderly sequence, and that children do not organize and use language as adults do, is evident in children's language production (Brown, 1973; Brown & Bellugi, 1964; Cazden, 1975; Menyuk, 1971). Adult attempts to direct language learning by telling and correcting usually meet with little success.

> Child: Nobody don't like me.
> Parent: No, say "Nobody likes me."
> Child: Nobody don't like me.
> Parent: No, Nobody likes me!
> (Seven more repetitions of this)
> Parent: No! Now listen carefully!
> Say "Nobody likes me!"
> Child: Oh! Nobody don't likes me. (McNeill, 1966)

Children learn language subconsciously, inductively, and by trial and error, rather than by repeated conscious practice of the more perfect language productions of adults (Moffett & Wagner, 1976). The natural language learning strategies (hypothesis test) children employ allow for examination of language features, for construction and testing of abstract patterns or rules that govern language behavior. Though children's language learning may appear to the casual adult observer to be accidental, haphazard, and in need of specific direction, children are proceeding toward language mastery deliberately, logically, and systematically.

Adult-conceived programs of sequenced language skills and subskills, satisfactory to the adult requirement for order and adequately reflecting adult awareness of language structure and function, cannot approximate children's maps of language and linguistic operations. What is sensible to the adult—the study and practice of bits and pieces of language and the application of rules to build whole languages—is not compatible with the children's own strategies. Children learn to be skillful with language by hearing, playing with, and using whole, meaningful language in meaningful contexts, and not by studying about language.

Access and Awareness

The systematic analyses to which children subject language result first in language facility, or linguistic access—the ability to process language. Children's trial-and-error methodology operates without need of metalinguistic awareness, the capacity to know about language and to consciously treat language as an object of study. Moreover, the acquisition and development of access seem to be prerequisites to the development of awareness (Biber, Cazden, & Franklin, 1975). Awareness of language as objects grows gradually—supported by children's increasing facility with language, related to their play with language—and, along with access, is a product of the trial-and-error process of language learning. Requiring that children learn, understand, and apply adult language rules for the purposes of developing language facility reverses the natural "access first" order of children's language development, and shortcuts the trial-and-error process without satisfactory results. Children's organization of language is, as suggested earlier, essentially immune to adult interference. When children begin to display metalinguistic awareness, that awareness will also be child-like, not adult-like (Cazden, 1975).

When children are ready to study language, appropriate awareness-producing activities can be found. But before children can understand a feature or operation of language, they must be able to produce that language. Though language study will produce conscious insight into the working of language, it will not necessarily result in an improvement in language facility (Combs, 1977; Cooper, 1973; O'Hare, 1971; Strong, 1973). Children's language growth is not always helped by or ready to benefit from adult levels of language organization and awareness (Piaget, 1973).

Meaning and Language Learning

Meaning is both substance and motivation for language use, as Watson shows in her article. Language is most often employed as a transparent vehicle for carrying meaning. A majority of language transactions commonly do not require conscious attention to and awareness of language shape and rules in operation. (Even language study itself requires the service of language as a vehicle to examine language as subject matter.) Children learn to manipulate and to control language by using it to think, to communicate, and to examine ideas important to them. Opportunity to use language as a tool with which to focus upon content provides the requisite conditions for the operation of natural language learning strategies, since language ability is acquired without benefit of informal language study. Facility with language is best achieved when language is used for the study of nonlinguistic subject matter (Moffett & Wagner, 1976; Postman & Weingartner, 1966). Language is first and most often a medium, second and more rarely a subject matter (Moffett & Wagner, 1976).

Integrating the Language Arts for Language Learning

In view of the above considerations, it would seem reasonable to allow the natural language learning strategies and needs of children to direct the shaping of programs and practices in language teaching. It would seem unreasonable to assume that 5, 6, or even 16 year olds are adults in their abilities to perceive, organize, and use language as do adults who study language.

Since child language learning requires situations for language use that could be called integrated, that is, language acts in which language use is directed toward topics of importance to the child and away from language study per se, organizing language teaching for such meaningful use of whole language would seem to accommodate the language learning needs and habits of children.

Integration of the language arts, despite methodological disagreement regarding the nature of integration in practice, amounts to keeping whole things whole and in the natural state, and to combining already whole things with other already whole things. Integrated language instruction involves combining the otherwise separately treated language arts subject matters into an interacting and mutually supporting experience, its foundation being language use. Perhaps the most useful guidelines for determining the workability of any integrated language arts activity designed for classroom use could be developed from what is known to be required for the trial-and-error strategy to proceed and from direct observation of the language production abilities and learning interests of the children.

Children's own readiness will govern their choice of language forms to be learned. In the context of a learning activity which requires the integrated use of many language arts, children are able to make a selection of language forms and skills to practice (test) which are compatible with their own language development. Many integrated activities might, for instance, be built around a literary theme and include, as natural and necessary elements in developing a variety of themes, related materials and ideas and language use tasks. If students compile a slang dictionary by interviewing others to determine meaning, nature, and extent of usage of slang terminologies, all of the language arts are pressed into sevice. A group of students who develop scripts and present readers theater, whether they adapt stories to script or develop their own material, must use many language skills in an integrated fashion. Though special attention might be given to individual language development tasks within the larger framework of the overall activity (i.e., student generated spelling word boxes or list), all individual language use tasks focus on the larger end product, theme, dictionary, theater presentation.

Once children's own language learning needs are accommodated in any given integrated experience with language, how the integration is accomplished and precisely what is done and in what order may not be as critical as the act of integration itself. It is the breadth of choice of language form and skill provided in the holistic and integrated language activity that accommodates the activity simultaneously to the different and special needs of many children.

Developing an Integrated Preservice Program

Preservice students quite naturally develop a catalog of ought-to-be's in educational practice, founded upon the attitudes and beliefs of those responsible for their teacher training.

Preservice students are overwhelmingly influenced by teaching methods and teaching materials, patterns of organization for courses, assignment making, evaluation, and testing procedures. When teachers of teachers say, "Go thou forth and do as I say, not as I do," most preservice students will do what they have seen and experienced, not what they have been told they should do. They are very much affected in their ability to learn by the way in which they are taught. Concerns for student centered, access first, inductive, holistic, integrated experiences, experiences which develop readiness, are just as applicable to adult learners as they are to children. What, though, do many of the adult students experience during teacher training?

The average preservice training sequence in the language arts is fragmented into single courses which treat language acquisition, language arts (writing, talking, listening, spelling, penmanship, grammar), literature, and reading as separate subject matters. Language acquisition can be further subdivided into early/later and normal/deviant acquisition; language arts into a variety of language activity and language study courses; literature into oral, written, children's and adolescent; and reading into numerous highly specialized offerings. Reading courses are often housed within a reading center or department and may equal or exceed in number all other language arts related courses combined. But literature, language acquisition, and language arts courses do not necessarily belong to the jurisdiction of the reading program. These others can be found within departments of English, general education, methods, communication arts, library, science, and special education, reflecting fragmentation by course prefix, course title and description, course scheduling, and the physical separation in the catalog.

Although some of the courses which fit the categories of language acquisition, language arts, reading, and literature might be necessary for indepth treatments of specific topics, the overall effect of separation suggests to the student that these language arts topics are indeed separate subject matters. Can preservice students who experienced such fragmentation be faulted for concluding that fragmentation is right and natural, and that similar separations of language related subject matters are proper for the public school classroom?

The fragmented organizations of language arts related subject matters to which many preservice students are exposed may indeed suggest to students that 1) reading is not a language art; 2) children's literature is not a language art; 3) language acquisition and development are not language arts; 4) writing, listening, talking, spelling, penmanship, and grammar are separate language arts subject matter; 5) reading is a separate subject matter and should be accorded more classroom time than all other language arts combined; 6) teaching reading in isolation of the other language use activities is a necessary, required procedure. Such fragmented approaches in higher education can produce teachers who say, "I don't have time for writing," or "I can't do anything with children's books this week; I have to get to page 35 in the blue workbook." Teachers cannot be expected to know what integration might be in its execution if they do not experience it as students. How, then, might teachers of teachers organize the various contents of language arts offerings in order to demonstrate an integration of the language arts?

A Model for Integrating the Elementary Preservice Language Arts Program

One effective method for integrating the language arts at the preservice level is through the design of a "block course" which brings together the separate course contents of reading, language arts, literature, and language acquisition along with provision for in-the-classroom teaching experiences. Within the time allotted for its execution, this rather massive block should attempt at all levels to model the integration of its component subject matters. A block course which simply brings together a collection of separate courses, then provides for continued separation (but within a more concentrated block of time) is not integrated. Teaching methods employed within such a block should also be designed to replicate methods recommended for the public school classroom.

The following discussion and figures provide one illustration of a block design for 12 quarter hours of integrated preservice teacher training coursework in reading, language, and children's literature. This specific 12 quarter hour block assumes five hours of coursework per day, three days a week, for approximately ten weeks.

Putting information about language learning into practice in higher education requires thinking about, organizing for, and presenting language arts content and methods in an integrated fashion. Such an investment of time and energy to change practice is difficult. Yet, if teacher perception of the integrated nature of language arts in the public school classroom is dependent upon preservice teacher experiences with integrated practices, then development of integrated approaches to language teaching/learning in teacher training programs would seem the sensible and necessary choice.

The Block Design

The language block is divided into four major areas of concentration: Developing Oral Language, Developing Written Language in Transition to Writing, Developing Written Language in Transition to Reading, and Developing Language in the Content Area. Each of the omnibus topics includes discussions and activities relating to appropriate considerations: aspects of theory and general background, development of readiness, assessment of abilities, integration of the other language arts, identification of and teaching of language skills in whole language contents, building access to and awareness of language form, examination of selected methods and materials, evaluation techniques, construction of nonlinguistic content-focused language teaching exercises, specific in-the-classroom teaching assignments (see Figures 1-4). The order of the subtopics listed in the figures is not critical, although topics often do follow in spontaneous and natural sequence when fitted within the larger frame of reference of organizing and managing the classroom to integrate the language arts.

Figure 1. Developing Oral Language: Related Content*

1. Language Acquisition—Natural Strategies and Processes
2. Language Access/Metalinguistic Awareness
3. Examining the Surface Features of Child Language
4. Syntactic and Semantic Maturity
5. Dialects and Dialect Differences
6. Building Expectations for Written Language Form
7. Foundations for Reading Readiness
8. Print Awareness, Memory Support Reading
9. Talking/Listening
   - autobiographical
   - data collection
   - data organization
   - reporting
   - language play
10. Using the Oral Literature
    - literary play
    - dramatic play and improvisation
    - language play—old and new inventions
    - the special oral literature of children
    - storytelling and other literary exercises
    - children as storytellers
    - chanting and charting
    - poetry
    - language/music connections
11. Using the Written Literature
    - reading aloud
    - dramatic play
    - Readers Theater
    - listening/talking centers
    - Mother Goose (transcribed collections)

*Topics listed above are not necessarily given in order of presentation or in order of importance. Topics themselves tend to integrate and are additionally nested within the larger focus on classroom organization and management. Not all topics appropriate to each of the four general areas described in Figures 1-4 are included.

Figure 2. Developing Written Language in Transition to Writing Related Content

1. Minimizing the Differences
2. Creating Print Environments
3. Bookmaking
4. Copywork
5. Taking and Giving Dictation
6. Data Collections
7. Charting
8. Listening to Written Language/Building Expectations for the Shapes of Written Language
9. Script and Story Writing
10. Making Song Language
11. Autobiographical Writing
12. Making Poetry
13. Teacher-coached Writing
14. Prewriting Activities
15. Notetaking and Keeping Journals and Notebooks
16. Researching and Data Collecting
17. Organizing and Charting Data for Writing
18. Writing Centers
19. Uninterrupted Sustained Silent Writing
20. Writing the Oral Literature/Transcriptions and Play
21. Approaches to Evaluation of Student Writing
    - setting criteria
    - building editing power
    - a place for handwriting, spelling, mechanics, punctuation
22. Developing Syntactic Maturity
    - talking and writing sentence expansions
    - substitution play
    - pattern writing
    - structural manipulations
    - sentence combining
23. Formal Language Study
24. Examining and Describing Language Forms and Behaviors
    - making dictionaries and "grammars"
    - word study and conscious word play
    - learning to describe subconscious rule formations

Figure 3. Developing Written Language in Transition to Reading Related Content

1. Acquisition Strategies and Processes
2. Writing Down/Reading Talk
3. Building Expectation Capacities
4. Building Home and Parent Support
5. Access/Awareness and Learning to Read
6. Views of Reading Process
7. Aspects of Comprehension
8. Aspects of Skill Teaching
9. "Official" Approaches
10. Other Approaches
11. Holistic Methodologies
12. Utilizing Student Writing
13. Using the Literature, Oral and Written
14. Incorporating Dramatic Activity
15. Using Content Area Topics
16. Using Literary Topics
17. Assessing Reading Ability
    evaluative measures
    observation of student reading behaviors
    planning for groups and individuals
18. Reading Programs
19. Managing/Expanding upon and Deviating from the Basal
20. About Mastery and Levels of Competence
21. About Accountability
22. Assessing Readiness at All Levels

Figure 4. Development of Language in the Content Area: Related Content

1. Nonlinguistic Content and Language From in Content Area Teaching—Some Relationships
2. Building Expectations for Content Area Language
3. Building Abilities to Control and Manipulate Content Area Written Materials
4. Talking/Writing in the Content Area
5. Using Content Related Literature, Oral and Written
6. Content Area Centers
7. Assessing Content Area Reading Materials
8. Assessing Student Ability to Read Content Area Materials
9. Accommodating Teaching to Student Ability
10. Grouping for Content Area Teaching
11. Building Study Skills and Strategies
12. Content Area Researching/Data Collection/Reporting
13. Content Area Related Problem Setting and Solving
14. Student Content Area Projects and Language Development
15. Literature as Content Area—Thematic Units
    observations: teaching literary awareness
    teaching appreciation of literature

Organization of topics with each of the four major areas is controlled or driven by exercises in examining and developing models for classroom organization and management, and by building teaching units fitted to one of the general models studied. Each of the four areas—oral language development (talking, listening), writing, reading, and content area—provides a language process focus for teaching around which integration of the language arts can be accomplished.

Within each general process focus, many more specific activities, topics, or central concerns can be identified about which integration can occur. While each such concentration of focus necessarily narrows the range of language development tasks which can be undertaken, each also provides opportunity for development of units which reintegrate specific language and/or content products. Topic related content and skills are taught and learned during unit building (each student constructs one fully integrated unit for each topic area), and smaller assignments are given in order to build skills and language as needed. Students do one integrated lesson per topic area in a public school classroom and learn to map classroom organization and management patterns on site. Student assignments are presented to the students in task analysis form; students thus learn to develop task analyzed activities for children. Many of the activities introduced in class are in continuous use beginning with the time of introduction.

Student assignments are not graded. Each is evaluated against specific criteria having to do with language control, completeness, degree of understanding of principle(s) involved, and excellence of execution. Students may repeat and/or revise work until they demonstrate required abilities and understanding. Ultimate learning and the development of the ability to self-assess are more important than grading degrees of perfection. There are no formal graded tests; however, each student is tested many times over. Evaluative student-teacher conferences occur when needed, and students whose own language skills need improvement and practice simultaneously work with an on-campus Reading/Writing Skills Development facility.

The integrated block design presented here is only one way of giving preservice students an integrated and generally holistic experience in learning. It is an exercise in time, space, student, and content management and it requires greater overall control than do separate subject matter courses in reading, literature, and language arts. But because of its organization of content within content, and the use to which it puts student learning, it is a means by which students gain a more complete perspective of the relationships between theory and practice. The block design provides a clear need to use and learn to control language that is directed to product rather than process. Figure 5 lists some of the specific activities (units) for integrated language teaching possible within each of the four general topic areas.

To provide students with patterns of classroom organization and management suitable to executing such integrated units in the classroom, select numbers of management models are presented. Students build and organize activity/topic/content teaching units to fit given management models and learn to manipulate the models to suit unit requirements. The models encourage students to plan for whole class, small group, individual activity work, and/or teacher instruction; for movement of children within the classroom; for center development and use; for utilization of space, time, and resource materials; and for general scope and sequence. Within each model, students can allow for skill teaching and student evaluation, and can integrate many language activities.

As students work within the frameworks of the organization and management models to construct product-focused units for language teaching, they are acquiring both information and skill. (Figures 1-4 point to those things that students learn to do while their attention is given to the larger tasks of making units and operating management models.) The block model described is organized in a nested fashion, one student task accomplished with the framework of another. As Figure 6 shows, the classroom organization and management models govern or "drive" the block design. The four general topic areas provide a convenient breakout of language processes, primarily in order to allow for the integrated teaching of the language arts and related content.

Figure 5. Possible Units for Integrated Language Teaching

Developing Oral Language	Developing Written Language in Transition to Writing	Developing Written Language in Transition to Reading	Developing Content Area Language
1. storytelling	1. bookmaking	1. literary theme and/or problem solving	1. content area topic center
2. the oral literature	2. library making	2. specific genre	2. critical issue centered
3. language play	3. topic-specific researching and data collection	3. author(s)	3. literary theme
4. creative dramatics and improvisations	4. script writing	4. historical/period	4. vocabulary development
5. topic-specific oral data collections	5. story writing	5. critical issue	5. study skills
6. children as storytellers	6. poem making	6. nonfiction topic	
7. Mother Goose—focuses and uses	7. writing for dramatic activity	7. fiction type	
8. poetry	8. autobiographical writing	8. special student interest	
9. literary theme	9. general composition writing	9. media	
10. song/riddle/rhyme/joke collections and play	10. dictionary making		
11. autobiographical data collection and talk	11. language study		
12. talking from experience/artifact	12. children as authors		
	13. journal keeping		
	14. collections and notebooks		
	15. newspaper making		

Figure 6. Overall Block Design

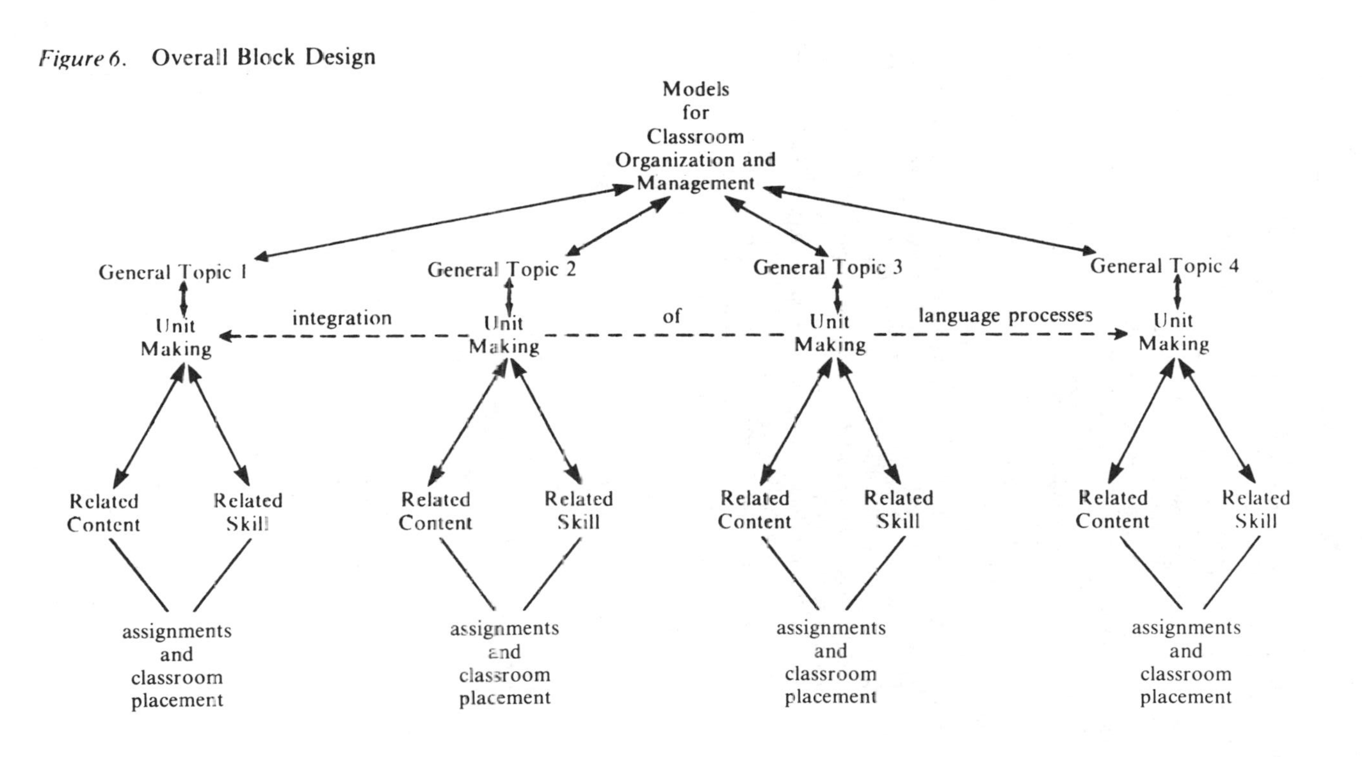

References

Biber, Barbara. Awareness in the learning process: A comment. In Charlotte B. Winsor (Ed.), *Dimensions of language experience.* New York: Agathon Press, 1975.

Brown, Roger. *A first language: The early stages.* Cambridge, Massachusetts: Harvard University Press, 1973.

Brown, Roger, & Bellugi, Ursula. Three processes in the child's acquisition of syntax. *Harvard Educational Review*, 1964, *34*, 133-51.

Cazden, Courtney B. Play with language and metalinguistic awareness: One dimension of language experience. In Charlotte B. Winsor (Ed.), *Dimensions of language experience.* New York: Agathon Press, 1975.

Combs, Warren E. Sentence combining practice aids reading comprehension. *Journal of Reading*, 1977, *21*, 18-24.

Cooper, Charles R. An outline for writing sentence-combining problems. *English Journal*, 1973, *62*, 96-102.

Franklin, Margery B. Aspects of symbolic functioning in childhood. In Charlotte B. Winsor (Ed.), *Dimensions of language experience.* New York: Agathon Press, 1975.

McNeill, David. Developmental psycholinguistics. In Frank Smith & George A. Miller (Eds.), *The genesis of language: A psycholinguistic approach.* Cambridge, Massachusetts: MIT Press, 1966.

Menyuk, Paula. *The acquisition and development of language.* Englewood Cliffs, New Jersey: Prentice-Hall, 1971.

Moffett, James, & Wagner, Betty J. *Student centered language arts and reading, K-13: A handbook for teachers.* Boston: Houghton Mifflin, 1976.

O'Hare, Frank. *Sentence combining: Improving student writing without formal grammar instruction.* Urbana, Illinois: National Council of Teachers of English, 1971.

Piaget, Jean. *The child and reality: Problems of genetic psychology.* New York: Penguin Books, 1973, 1976.

Postman, Neil, & Weingartner, Charles. *Linguistics: A revolution in teaching.* New York: Dell, 1966.

Strong, William. *Sentence combining: A composing book.* New York: Random House,

Part Three
Classroom Practices

Bringing Together Reading and Writing

Dorothy J. Watson
University of Missouri at Columbia

Reading and writing have to do with meaning and with people—their languages, their intentions, their expectations, and the situations in which they find themselves. Eight year old Angela tacitly understands this and, therefore, is an easy receiver and producer of meaningful messages. For example, when the need arose within a social context to convey a personal message to her brother (who needed to be reminded of the virtues of tidiness), Angela chose language that represented her meaning (reality), and wrote Rules in the Bathroom.

When the receiver of this message, 4 year old Matthew, saw his sister's note taped to the bathroom door he had no doubt that the message was for him. And he was able to accurately predict its content. The lesson Matthew learned from this experience was not the one Angela hoped for (the bathroom wasn't much tidier after his visits). Rather, Matthew learned about language and its use: someone intended to tell me something; under similar circumstances someone had sent this message to me before—orally; someone was now sending the message by way of paper and magic marker; the content of the written message will be like the content of the oral message; the conventions of the oral message (loud talk accompanied by finger shaking, foot stomping, and calling in Mother) are different from the conventions of the written message (print, numbers, lines, spaces, words, sentences, punctuation marks, and quiet); reading and writing, like speaking and listening, are useful tools.

RULES in the Bathroom

1. If you make a mess please clean it up. for the other Person!
2. If you know who made a mess ether clean it up, or tell him
3. flush the tolet
4. Make shure that the Bathroom is redy for others.
5. Tell somone if you made a mess.
6. Don't tell lies about the bathroom. (like if you made a mess and said you didn't)
7. If you had an acadent don't be scard tell my mom. (donna) and shell clean it up.
8. Dont thow Wet things like wet towls.
9. Dont Pont your middle finger at God. (of corse!)
10. if you dont like a rule tell me.
11. Follow these rules.
12. have a happy day every one even God!

Angela
7 yrs. 11 mo.

Using the above as preface, it is the intention of this paper to do two things. First, to build on the functional view of oral language acquisition and its relationship to reading and writing presented by Crafton earlier in this volume. This will be done by focusing on the two processes as mutually supportive linguistic social systems. And second, to suggest classroom activities, consistent with the theoretical base presented, that will advance reading and writing processes.

The following model may help us with both tasks. It is a compilation of several notions about language and language users that includes the following: language is social and learned in the context of meaningful situations (Halliday, 1975); language users receive and produce information and perceive both language processes to be active (Goodman, 1982; Graves, 1983); and active writers *intend* certain meanings and use certain conventions while active readers *expect* certain meanings and certain conventions (Smith, 1982).

In this model we see that the language processes of listening, reading, speaking, and writing are developed and practiced in the sociolinguistic settings of home, school, and community, all of which are embedded in and influenced by the culture of the language user. Undergirding this is the assertion that reading, like listening, involves anticipating meanings and conventions. Such expectations guide the reader in the selection of on-the-page and off-the-page cues that lead to constructing a message. Writing is similar to speaking in that it involves wishing to say something and then producing cues for someone else to use in resolving that intention. Reading is basically receptive, writing basically expressive, but both are transactive. That is, in both there is a lively negotiation between the writer and the unseen reader, or between the reader and the unseen writer in which the potential of both writer and reader is affected. Writers broaden the potential of their readers if they are aware of their audience's life and linguistic backgrounds and then use language and conventions that take advantage of the reader's knowledge. Readers affect the text potential when they bring appropriate life and linguistic experiences to the passage. Certain texts can shrink the potential of the readers, making them appear to be poor readers. Certain readers can diminish the potential of a text, making the text appear to be poorly written. On the other hand, when readers with background knowledge and reading strategies that push toward the construction of meaning come to well written text, the potential seems limitless. Reading and writing are transactive processes that involve action and change of both text and reader (Rosenblatt, 1978).

Our next consideration is the contexts of situations in which these transactions occur. Like listening and speaking, reading and writing are acquired because they are functional and because they occur in meaningful social settings. As children play and work with others in their societies of home, school, and community, they find it necessary to express their meanings for a

variety of reasons and in a variety of ways. Crafton discusses seven functions through which a child acquires oral language or, as Halliday puts it, "learns how to mean." These seven functions have inspired others (Goodman & Goodman, 1976) to draw parallel functional motivations for learning to read. A third parallel follows easily—motivations for learning to write. Halliday's categories are appealing because they give teachers an idea of the underlying forces (I want, do as I tell you, tell me why) that motivate children into the sociolinguistic acts of reading and writing. That is, we can easily see how natural it is (follows directly from a functional motivation) for children to write and read notes, signs, letters, rules, autobiographies, language experience stories, and newspaper articles. Halliday's point (1978) is important:

> We do not experience language in isolation—if we did we would not recognize it as language—but always in relation to a scenario, some background of persons and actions and events from which the things which are said derive their meaning. This is referred to as the "situation" so language is said to function in "contexts of situations" and any account of language which fails to build in the situation as an essential ingredient is likely to be artificial and unrewarding.

Returning to the model, two points need to be considered, as they directly affect reading and writing instruction. The first has to do with the use of visual cues in reading and writing. These visual cues include letters and combinations of letters, punctuation marks, italics, lowercase and uppercase print, and even the white spaces between words. Strangely, this utilitarian, surface-level, information-relating system of the language can present major problems for the reader and writer—if it becomes the focus of instruction. Warning against such a visual emphasis, Smith (1972) suggests that if writing is seen as a matter of reproducing letters, and reading as a matter of identifying them, then mastery of phonics can become the goal of reading instruction; and precision in spelling, letter formation, or filling the page with print can become the prevailing concern of writing lessons. This kind of "alphabetic puritanism" neglects the meaningful intent of writers and the meaningful expectations of readers, and is a prime bone of contention for educators who are disturbed by the misplaced emphasis of "back to basics" proponents.

The second issue raised by the "integrated language arts" section of the model has to do with the order in which children acquire language modes. The model challenges the notion that children learn to write only after they have listened, spoken, and read. Current research (Clay, 1975; Goodman & Cox, 1978; Harste, Burke & Woodward, 1981; King, 1979; Wiseman, 1979) indicates that children can experiment with writing as soon as they can hold a pencil or make marks in sand. In a 1976 conference on reading, Carol Chomsky gave accounts of children who were writing—using invented spellings—before they knew how to read. Chomsky argued that expecting children to read before they write is an imposition that hinders their willing involvement in language and takes the fun out of learning. Ferreiro and Teberosky (1982) add that if children are to understand the writing system of their culture, they must be able to do more than name letters and utter sounds. Ferreiro and Teberosky say children must actively construct the writing system—by writing. If children become authors as they become readers, they discover through experience that writing and reading are related, with meaning and use as the link between them. To children who learn the processes simultaneously, print is no mystery and requires no manipulation (sounding out, dividing words into syllables, finding *the* main idea) to be understood. Authors are the first readers of their own work. Children who write messages they perceive to be sensible are not likely to accept nonsense when they encounter the work of other authors. They expect their own print to have a semantic intent and they will demand it of others.

Read's landmark research (1975) provides insights into the phenomenon of preschool and kindergarten children's learning to spell. The invented spellings of these young children reveal their intuitive strategies: they discover that a letter (often from their own names) can spell a sound, and they begin to spell words based on the sounds contained within the letter names (for instance, if the letter *h* contains the /ch/, then the invented spelling for *chair* for some children would logically begin with the letter *h*). If, as Read indicates, the spelling creations of children are not whimsical and haphazard but, instead, are indicative of their sophisticated understanding of phonology, and if these spellings can in fact be categorized, then it seems reasonable for teachers to encourage their students to use spelling variations. This does not mean we are not interested in standard spelling. It means that our first interest is to encourage children to express meaning—reality. Standard spelling will develop as children are more and more actively involved in using language through reading and writing.

Just as children are encouraged to use what they know about life and language when they read, they are encouraged to do the same thing when they write. Six year old Tracy does exactly that when, while waiting to see the nurse, she writes in her journal:

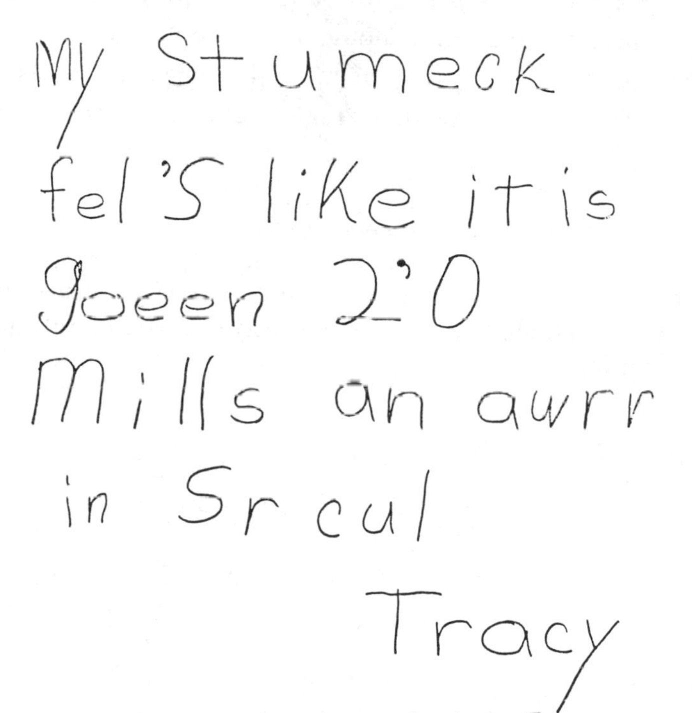

My stomach feels like it is going
twenty miles an hour in circles.

Tracy has a message and she uses her knowledge of speech sounds and print to invent spellings so that her message can be written.

Proficient readers and writers consider all the pragmatic and linguistic information available to them. Earlier, Crafton discussed the graphophonemic, grammatical, and semantic systems available to children. If for any reason one of the systems is not used, the process may falter, stop or end in nonsense. The following example indicates that Jane (age 10) was attending to the graphophonemic system (making letter-sound matches) while ignoring other important linguistic cues. Her miscues are written above the typescript.

> There will be prizes for children who take the
> best pictures. You should see those prizes.
> All the family stood around him when the prints
> were done. How they laughed at some of the
> pictures!

Sammy (age 8), who was asked to write about a class trip, neglected to use the grammar of language as a frame for his meaning. He elected simply to list correctly spelled words. Because he avoided grammatical structures, we can only guess at his meaning.

Zoo Trip

Yesterday	Animals	Feed	Tigers
Zoo	Zebra	Jump	Fun

If we compare Sammy's "story" with Angela's Rules in the Bathroom and with Tracy's journal notation, we can infer that intention and instruction may be the keys to what and how children write. If Sammy had a purpose in his writing, he was unable to make it known to his readers because his writing instruction seems to have focused mainly on correct spelling and neat handwriting. Angela and Tracy intended to get their meanings across and they were encouraged to use language to do it.

Activities that Bring Together Reading and Writing

The second purpose of this paper is to present activities that are compatible and consistent with what we know about language and language users, and that will support both the reading and writing processes. The activities mentioned are but a few in which the student can be author and reader, producer and receiver of messages.

Books without Words

When asked, children will explain that books without words, unlike their other picture books, "don't have any writing in them." Such an oversight encourages children to become authors and to share their stories with others. After children give voice to their story, they write their own text or dictate it to the teacher. The story is then clipped to the appropriate page. Some particularly good wordless books for this activity are *Bobo's Dream* by Martha Alexander, *Look What I Can Do* by Jose Aruego, *What Whiskers Did* by Ruth Carroll, *The Chicken's Child* by Margaret Hartelius, and all of Mercer Mayer's excellent books without words. Richard Abrahamson in his "An Update on Wordless Picture Books with an Annotated "Bibliography" (1981) gives us information on high quality books without words. Books with good illustrations but with meager texts ("Mat sat on the cat.") can also be used if a teacher will snip off or cover up the "nontext" and then ask children to write real stories.

Bringing Familiar Language into the Classroom

Children's familiar language appears in many forms: jump rope rhymes, cheerleading yells, songs, sayings, poems, jokes, riddles, commercials, and family stories. Children enjoy writing and illustrating their own familiar language to the teacher, who writes it on the board. Everyone reads it and adds it to their own and to the class book. Following is one of Greg's first writing ventures, language so familiar that it had to be shared, said, written, read, and even acted out.

Aviance Night!

Ive ben sweet and
Ive ben good had a
whole day of mother
hood but I
have gunu
a aveance night

Greg

Written Conversations

Written conversations are pen and paper talk between a teacher and a student in which the teacher initiates the conversation by writing a message to the student. The student reads the message and writes a reply. Sometimes it is necessary to read the dialogue to the student, but as the conversation becomes more predictable, the student usually will not need this help. The following is a conversation between a teacher and a first grader.

Your baby rabbits are so cute! Thank you for bringing them. How are they today?

They are fin How are your KIDS

One girl is not feeling very well but the other one is fine. She is singing in a play tomorrow night

That is nis

What are you doing today? Weeken

What are you working on? week

What work?

(working ON deT TadeTs

Where did you get dot to dots?

FROM YOU

Me! No! I don't remember that. What else are you doing? a POTea

What is the poster about? me

What does it tell about you? I'm a semr

What else? a diver

How did you learn to dive?

all You GaT To do is Jeeaq

It would scare me to jump. Do you jump off a high board? yes

You're brave! What do you like to do most of all? Peiy

What do you play?

Fello The leTr

Who do you play follow the leader with?

My Fecs

Kyle & K. Copeland
Grade 1, January

Children quickly get the knack of such conversations and begin pen and paper discussions with their classmates. Some students are so proficient with written conversations that they can keep two going simultaneously. As teachers get the hang of good questioning techniques, they can explore feelings as well as elicit language from their students. The following is a junior high student's discussion with her teacher.

Laurie, why didn't you ask for a headset today?

becuase i wasn't in a mood today.

What kind of mood are you in today?

A stopey mood today.

Why do you feel this way?

becuse i sleep on the wrong side

What is your wrong side?

the side that i feld of.

When did you fall off?

last night.

Does it still hurt?

no

Are you feeling better now?

Yes.

That's good!

Yes

Are you ready to work again?

Yes

What are you going to do?

Big Bill

Laurie and Mrs. Ijitom
Title I, Jr Hi.

These pen and paper conversations tacitly point up the similarities and differences between oral and written language. The written conversation necessitates some editing of the oral message—you simply don't/can't write down everything you might include in an oral conversation. Carolyn Burke and her students at Indiana University have developed this activity for use with very young children as well as adults (King, 1983).

Extended Literature

The world of children's stories and books is a natural source for the integration of the language arts. One example will sufficiently illustrate the point. Stephen Kellogg's *Can I Keep Him*? (a favorite of Jane Decker's Title I reading students) tells the story of a small boy's attempts to talk his mother into letting him keep (among other animals) a dog, a fawn, a bear, and a python. His mother persistently refuses him, each time providing a reasonable argument, such as, "No, dear. Tigers grow up to have terrible appetites. They eat enormous amounts of food, and sometimes they eat people. We could never afford to feed a tiger." In addition to delightful illustrations and a captivating story, Stephen Kellogg provides the repetitive refrain, "Can I keep him?" for beginning readers to chant. This unambiguous, predictable sentence allows insecure readers to participate in reading the story.

Decker's first and second graders loved *Can I Keep Him*? and used it as a model to write their own letters asking if they could bring animals to reading class. Decker's replies to each student were read, shared, and reread. The treasured letters were collected and compiled, and now a new book, *Can I Bring Him to Reading*? is a class favorite.

Dear Mrs. Pecker
I have a dog and I want
to bring him to reading. He will
not runaround and he will not
bark and he will not clime on nobody
can I bring him to reading.

Renee
Grade 2

Dear Renee,

No, you cannot bring your dog to reading. I'm sure he would not bark, climb on anyone, or run around, but dogs have tails. Tails knock books and papers on the floor.

Mrs. Decker

Language Experience

Children experience, talk about their experiences, and then write about them, with the help of a "talking secretary." Teachers serve as talking secretaries as they urge authors to clarify their thoughts by asking questions that a potential reader might ask, and by simply listening and responding to the telling of the author's experiences. Talking secretaries never control the composing process. This tried and proven language experience activity is a basic in promoting the writer as reader and the reader as writer. And, because there are no sociopsycholinguistic gaps between the writer and the reader, there are no roadblocks in the construction of meaning. This is not to say that students can always reread what they have written. They may need to consider again their motivation for writing, what they intended to say and what they wrote first; in other words, they may need to reconstruct the original writing experience in order to read their own composition.

The question of how a teacher structures class activities so as to have time to respond in writing to children's writing, or to engage in written conversations with some of them, is addressed in Rhodes' paper later in this volume. In the kind of daily and weekly classroom schedule she proposes, there is enough time to go around—during the two one-hour work periods, while children are in music and PE, and after school. Time usually spent in round robin reading and workbook completion thus can be utilized more wisely with strategies suggested here.

Team Stories

Writing a text with a partner or as a member of a team provides a situation in which the strengths of individual members can support the entire team. As children discuss their story, they impose structure on it; that is, they use a grammatical frame. Brown (1977) suggests that this sense of story influences comprehension. Roulette stories are one form of team stories in which team writers don't discuss their text, but contribute to a growing discourse when it is their turn to do so. The readers/writers of the roulette story quickly see the need for links between their portion and the existing text, then the need for a plot and a central character emerge. These beginnings for group members can grow into individual creations with all the basic structuring principles of true narratives.

While walking home one moonlight night I had the feeling I was being followed. Shure enuff ever time I tok one little step I cold heâr this relley weerd sound. Well maybee you think I wasn't scard. Well I was and I took off so fast that I couldnt even see where I was going.

All of a suden I went splat!!!!! I ran into this man He was really mad. I thought he was going to kill me.

But he didn't. Ensted he said you are the fastest runer I know. I'm going to get you in the Olympicks

Jon, Paul, Cliff, Dave & Bud

Interviewing Friends

Students first discuss what they would like to know about other students and what they would like others to know about themselves. The teacher acts as a scribe, writing their interview questions on the board: What sports do you like best? What do you do on Saturday? What is your favorite book? How would you describe yourself? What are you afraid of? These and suitable follow-up questions help prepare for a productive interview.

Spontaneous and informal conversation precedes the interview as the partners take snapshots, draw pictures, or cut out silhouettes of each other. These pictures, often accompanied by fingerprints (another way of showing one's uniqueness), are placed on posterboard or on the cover of an individual's book (e.g., *The Biography of Tony Jones*). If a poster is made, some identifying characteristics and bits of information (has brown eyes, loves basketball, never misses "Mork and Mindy," read *Where the Red Fern Grows* five times) can be added and used by the partner when introducing the Student of the Day. If the interviewer decides to produce a book, chapters can be written by different class members (including the teacher), and one chapter might be an autobiographical frame in which the subject fills in the missing parts with details of his/her life. These pupil-produced books become an important part of the classroom library and are read and referred to again and again, an idea further developed by Ammon later in this volume.

Conclusion

The activities listed above are supportive of both reading and writing, and are consistent with the following notions about learners and their language:

1. Language is learned in meaning filled contexts by individuals who want and need to use it. In other words, the language an individual learns and uses must function in real social situations and must be important to the learner.

2. Reading and writing are transactions in which both the reader and writer are active and are capable of modifying each other's potential.

3. "Alphabetic puritanism," overattention to form, and isolated lessons in one of the language modes or in one of the language systems decompose language, and are nonfunctional and time consuming practices that can be referred to only as meaningless and defeating.

4. The processes of reading and writing can be learned simultaneously, each strengthening and supporting the other.

5. Readers and writers must concern themselves with meaning—both in receiving and in producing it. If there is no meaning there is no impetus for using language.

References

Abrahamson, Richard. An update on wordless picture books with an annotated bibliography. *Reading Teacher*, 1981, *34*, 417-421.

Brown, Ann. *Knowing when, where, and how to remember: A problem of metacognition* (Tech. Rep. No. 47). Center for the Study of Reading, Urbana-Champaign, 1977.

Chomsky, Carol. Approaching reading through invented spelling. Presented at the Conference on Theory and Practice of Beginning Reading Instruction. Learning Research and Development Center, University of Pittsburgh, May 1976.

Chomsky, Carol. Write first, read later. *Childhood Education*, 1971, *47*, 296-299.

Clay, Marie M. *What did I write?* Auckland, New Zealand: Heinemann Educational Books, 1975.

Decker, Jane, and her students. *Can I bring him to reading?* Columbia, Missouri: Grant Elementary School, 1979.

Ferreiro, Emilia, & Teberosky, Ana. *Literacy before schooling*. Exeter, New Hampshire: Heinemann Educational Books, 1982.

Goodman, Kenneth S. *Language and literacy: The selected writings of Kenneth S. Goodman*. Vols. 1 and 2. Edited by Frederick V. Gollasch. Boston: Routledge & Kegan Paul Ltd. 1982.

Goodman, K.S., & Goodman, Y. Learning to read is natural. Presented at the Conference on Theory and Practice of Beginning Reading Instruction. Learning Research and Development Center, University of Pittsburgh, April 1976.

Goodman, Yetta, & Cox, V. *The development of literacy in young children*. Basic Skills Group of National Institute of Education, 1978.

Graves, Donald H. *Writing: Teacher and children at work*. Exeter, New Hampshire: Heinemann Educational Books, 1983.

Halliday, M.A.K. *Language as social semiotic: The social interpretation of language and meaning*. Baltimore: University Park Press, 1978.

Halliday, M.A.K. *Learning how to mean: Explorations in the development of language*. London: Edward Arnold Ltd., 1975.

Harste, Jerome, Burke, Carolyn, & Woodward, Virginia. *Children, their language and world: Initial encounters with print*. National Institute of Education, 1981.

Kellogg, Stephen. *Can I keep him?* New York: Dial Press, 1971.

King, Dorothy. Burke's written conversation. In J. Collins (Ed.), *Teaching all children to write*. New York State English Council, 1983.

King, Martha. Toward a theory of early writing development. *Research in the Teaching of English*, 1979, *13*, 243-253.

Read, Charles. *Children's categorization of speech sounds in English*. Urbana, Illinois: National Council of Teachers of English, 1975.

Rosenblatt, Louise M. *The reader, the test, the poem*. Carbondale: Southern Illinois University Press, 1978.

Smith, Frank. Phonology and orthography: Reading and writing. *Elementary English*, 1972, *49*, 1075-1088.

Smith, Frank. *Writing and the writer*. New York: Holt, Rinehart & Winston, 1982.

Wiseman, Donna. *A psycholinguistic description of the reading and writing behavior of a selected group of five year old children*. Doctoral dissertation, University of Missouri at Columbia, 1979.

Organizing the Elementary Classroom for Effective Language Learning

Lynn K. Rhodes
University of Colorado at Denver

Educators often assume that the elementary school years must be devoted to direct instruction of language skills. Such an assumption is implied in much that is done in the schools. Large blocks of time are devoted to instruction of reading skills, spelling lists, handwriting, and grammar; the entire morning is usually scheduled for such instruction because that is when children are "fresh." The majority of special help pullout classes are language skill classes of various kinds, usually reading classes; there, children spend even more time in skill instruction. Little time is devoted to content area classes and these classes are often rotated—science is studied during one grading period and social studies the next. In many content area classes, particularly in primary grades, reading and writing are avoided in favor of alternate ways of presenting information. Art and music classes are viewed by teachers and students as "relief" time from learning language skills. Evaluation focuses on language skill ability: Can the child read, spell, and punctuate at grade level?

The effect of such a focus on language skills is devastating to some teachers and students—teacher and student burnout and disinterest, student failure, student inability to comprehend what has been read or to write so others can comprehend what has been written. The effect on other teachers and students is more subtle—they learn to play the game of school, but they don't become very involved with teaching or learning because they know that most of it has no relevance to the world outside the school.

This paper argues, instead, that language skills are best learned in the process of *using* language in all its expressions (speaking, listening, reading, and writing) in order to explore the world. In general, the ideas contained herein are based on the following language learning principles:

1. Children become effective language users by using language in a variety of meaningful and purposeful ways. That is, children learn to read and write and speak and listen by reading and writing and speaking and listening for functional purposes.
2. Language learning is personally important and concretely based. That is, children learn language by communicating with others about aspects of their world with which they can become involved and which they find intriguing and important to them.
3. Children utilize what they understand about their world and language in order to broaden and extend those understandings. In regards to language, current understanding of any expressions of language (reading, writing, speaking, listening), its functions, and its conventions, can be utilized by children in further developing other language expressions.

The principles outlined above can be summarized in one statement: language is learned by using it as a means to an end—to learn more about the world. Such a statement is in direct opposition to the assumption underlying much of the current language instruction in schools—that language is learned as an end in itself.

If effective language learning occurs while children use language as tools to learn about the world, a curricular vehicle must be utilized that will encourage exploration of the world through the use of reading, writing, listening, and speaking. Such a vehicle is the thematic unit, a type of curriculum that focuses on the exploration of a number of related concepts. The theme for the unit can be selected because it is a required curriculum topic, because the teacher knows that it will inspire the children's interest and fulfill some of their needs, or because the children themselves suggested it. The concepts to be studied within the thematic unit are selected with the children's interests and needs in mind; reading, writing, listening, and speaking are enlisted in integrated, purposeful, and meaningful ways in order to study the concepts.

This article is devoted to the concerns teachers have regarding the organization of an elementary classroom based on the beliefs about language learning reviewed earlier in this volume. Because the thematic unit provides the content to be explored, a sample thematic unit will be presented first, along with guidelines for preparing such a unit. Other suggestions will follow concerning grouping, scheduling, organizing classroom space, recruiting a variety of people as teachers, and evaluation. Once the thematic unit has been presented, the rationale for other suggestions will be apparent: why the schedule includes flexible "work periods," what the various suggested groups of children will do, why various kinds of floor spaces are advised, what types of learning and involvement might be evaluated, and how people other than a teacher can contribute to the classroom.

The Thematic Unit

Introduction

Since the primary grades are those that focus most heavily on skills instruction, a thematic unit has been selected for presentation that was written for children beginning first grade. The unit is entitled *A Lot Can Be Said about "Little"** and is intended "to give small children some big ideas about little things and their place in the world" (Hutchison, 1980).

It is not possible to present the entire "Little" unit here because it is extensive and, most important, it is not cast in stone; the teacher *and the children* who live with the ideas, lessons, and materials presented here will add, subtract, and adapt them. In other words, plans in a thematic unit are a point of departure. In fact, the teacher who wrote this unit remarked in her introduction to it, "Becoming involved with the children and materials usually suggests more and better ideas that can be thought of beforehand" (Hutchison, 1980).

*Thanks are extended to Janice Hutchison, a Denver Metro-area teacher, who wrote the "Little" unit and who willingly shared it.

Unit Concepts

The teacher's first consideration in planning a thematic unit is to list the major concepts to be explored by the children. Decisions can be made about resources, lessons, and activities once the concepts are outlined.

Four of the major concepts of *A Lot Can Be Said about "Little"* are:

1. Little fellows can make a big difference.
2. Little things can be the beginning of something much bigger or something new and different.
3. Biggest isn't always best.
4. Sometimes you have to make the best of being little.

These four concepts selected from the "Little" unit are quite broad. Note the difference between them and a concept taken from a more narrowly focused thematic unit on metamorphosis: "Inside a chrysalis, a caterpillar goes through a complete physical change before it emerges as a butterfly." As will be seen, the concept about metamorphosis is one that the children experiencing the "Little" unit will come to understand also; it is a part of what is explored within the broad second concept of the unit.

Some teachers prefer to prepare broadly based thematic units such as the "Little" unit; others prefer more narrowly focused units. In general, the more narrowly focused a unit is, the more units are necessary in the classroom at a given time. The broadly based unit permits more flexibility and creativity; "more and better ideas than can be thought of beforehand" can find their way to the surface. However, some teachers find that several more narrowly focused units are easier to plan and manage, and, they permit easier evaluation of student growth.

Resources for the Development of Concepts

In planning a thematic unit, the next step for many teachers is to gather some of the resources that children can use to explore the concepts; the resources themselves often provide ideas for lessons and activities. Some of the possible resource categories to be considered are: tradebooks, textbooks, films, filmstrips, records, picture files, community people and organizations, magazines, children's own work, professional references, and real world objects. A sampling of the resources available for the four "Little" unit concepts follows:

Little fellows can make a big difference.

- *The Great Big Enormous Turnip* (Tolstoy, 1972). In this story, a mouse helps a group of larger characters succeed in pulling up a huge turnip.
- *The Littlest Angel* (Tazewell, 1973). In this recording, the smallest and most mischievous angel in heaven delights God with his small earthly Christmas presents.
- *Lentil* (Weston Woods, 1957). A film about a small boy who succeeds in making a crotchety old man happy when no one else could. Also a tradebook by Robert McCloskey.

Little things can be the beginning of something bigger or something new and different.

- *Stone Soup* (Brown, 1947). When the townspeople pretend they have no food, three soldiers fool them into contributing various small bits of food to the water in which they are boiling stones, resulting in a wonderful soup.
- *Butterflies* (Mousdale, 1973). An easy-to-read explanation of the metamorphosis of butterflies and moths.
- A variety of seeds for experiments and planting.

Biggest isn't always best.

- "Children Can" (Rogers, 1972). This song reminds children they can do lots of things adults can't do or don't like to do.
- "The Biggest House in the World" (Channing, 1976). In this recording, a snail finds out that a small shell is more functional than a large one for seeing the world and eating.
- *Tikki Tikki Tembo* (Mosel, 1968). This is a story of why the Chinese give their children little, short names rather than big, long names.

Sometimes you have to make the best of being little.

- Children from the second grade who are willing to give the first graders advice on how to make the best out of their year in first grade.
- *If I had...* (Mayer, 1968). A small boy fantasizes about various creatures who can protect him from bigger boys who are bullies. He finally decides his big brother is his best bet.
- *Swimmy* (Connecticut Films, 1969). A film about a small fish who finds a way to live safely with the large fish in the sea. Also a tradebook by Leo Lionni.

Many children's books have been made into excellent recordings, films, and filmstrips (see *Swimmy* and *Lentil* above, as examples). Likewise, much of the science and social studies information children are interested in can be found in media other than books. Children enjoy the same story or information presented in a number of ways and this enjoyment can be used to advantage: reading and writing become more effective as children build more of a background in the subject matter.

Constructing Lessons and Activities

The next step in planning a thematic unit is to outline the lessons and activities that the children are to be involved in. For our purposes here, *lessons* are essentially teacher led or directed while *activities* may be handled fairly independently by the children. Depending on the children's backgrounds and abilities, it may be necessary for the teacher to introduce some or many of the activities in some detail prior to the children's independent involvement in them.

A sampling of some lessons and activities to teach each of the four selected "Little" unit concepts follows:

Little fellows can make a big difference.

- After the children have become familiar enough with *The Great Big Enormous Turnip* (Tolstoy, 1972) that most can read it (the story is highly predictable), the teacher can read *Elephant in a Well* (Ets, 1972) to the class and involve them in a discussion of the similarities and differences in the two stories. The themes, problems, and story structures are identical; differences lie in the characters involved.

- At least four stories in the unit have a mouse as a major character. Besides the two mentioned in the paragraph above, there is "The Little Mouse that Roared" (Barty, 1978) and "The Lion and the Mouse," an Aesop fable. In a learning center, the children can be asked to draw and write about their favorite mouse character for sharing later with the class. As an alternative, they can locate another book with a major mouse character and share it with the class.

- Groups of children can dramatize *Buzz, Buzz, Buzz* (Barton, 1973) and/or *The Bus Ride* (Scott, Foresman, 1971). Both are highly predictable books and a bee figures as the troublemaker in both.

Little things can be the beginning of something much bigger or something new and different.

- Following the reading of *Stone Soup* (Brown, 1947), the class can make a list of all the small bits of food contributed by the villagers to the soup. The soup can be recreated by the students on a hot plate after the ingredients have been brought to class. (Be sure to wash the stones well!) Following the activity, a language experience chart can be dictated in order to record the activity for a class history book. This can be the first in a long series of cooking activities.

- Fall is a good time to find caterpillars. And there are a number of books, both fiction and nonfiction, that detail the transformation of the caterpillar for young children. Some are: *The Very Hungry Caterpillar* (Carle, no date), *Butterflies* (Mousdale, 1973), and *Terry and the Caterpillars* (Selsam, 1962). Besides reading the books in order to discover how to care for the collected caterpillars, records can be kept, via group or individual drawings and writings, of the observation of the caterpillars. (The same activities can be done with tadpoles and ant colonies.)

- There is also a large number of books about seeds and their transformation into plants written for young children. Some are: *The Popcorn Book* (Scott, Foresman, 1971), *How a Seed Grows* (Jordan, 1960), *Fun Time Weird Gardens* (Yerian & Yerian, 1975), and *Seeds and More Seeds* (Selsam, 1959). All are full of ideas and experiments for children to carry out. Again, records should be kept via drawings and writing. Many seeds may be collected, labeled, drawn, and categorized in the fall.

Biggest isn't always best.

- As a follow-up to listening to "Children Can" (Rogers, 1972), ask the children to draw and write about something they can do that adults can't do because they are too big or that adults don't like to do because they are grown up.
- After listening to "The Biggest House in the World" (Channing, 1976), ask the children to draw and color what they think "the biggest house in the world" looked like. (It is described in several ways in the story.)
- Put some typical little things in a learning center (a feather, a grain of salt, a seed, a lightning bug, a pencil). Tell the children to choose one object and to imagine that all the same type of objects (all feathers, for example) were as big as children. Ask them to draw and write about how that would change how the object functions in the world.

Sometimes you have to make the best of being little.

- After listening to "You Can Never Go Down the Drain"

(Rogers, 1972), ask the children to write and draw about something that frightened them when they were small (or something that currently frightens a smaller brother or sister).

- After reading *If I Had* ...(Mayer, 1968), ask the children to write and illustrate a new episode involving the character in the book. After sharing the work, let the children choose the best ideas for inclusion in a new *If I had* ... book to be put in the class library.
- After reading *Inch by Inch* (Lionni, 1960), a story of an inch worm who gets out of tough situations by measuring things, ask the children to draw an inch worm to size. After it has been cut out, have the children estimate and then measure the lengths of a number of objects with their inch worm. The height of the children in the class and differences in heights can be expressed in "inch worms."

Grouping

For a number of years there has been a great deal of discussion about "individualized instruction." The basic tenet behind such a notion is that children's individual needs should be met, allowing children to learn what they need to learn about the world and communication in the world. Individualized instruction does *not* mean that each child must have one-on-one instruction or that each child in the room is working on a different assignment. It means that children are learning what they need to learn, are capable of learning, and are interested in learning. These conditions often can be met best in interaction with other people; interaction with others stimulates language use and growth.

Children, themselves, can often determine what they are capable of and interested in learning. For that reason, groupings can be decided upon by students alone, by students and teachers in concert, and infrequently by the teacher alone. Groupings vary in purpose, in size, and duration and should be fluid; the group's existence and composition should be reexamined frequently by the teacher and children involved. Some suggested groupings based on purpose follow.

Friendship groups are useful in many learning situations. A group writing conference, where the level of trust must be high and where various levels of ability are valuable, is an example of a situation in which they should be considered. The dramatization of *Buzz, Buzz, Buzz*, suggested in the thematic unit, could also be done by a group of friends.

Interest groups are useful when children want to explore the same topic together. For example, interest groups can be formed for reading a selected book. Six to eight paperback titles can be listed on the chalkboard for a week. At the end of the week, all children must have chosen one of the books to read and have indicated their choice by writing their names by the book on the chalkboard. Each resulting group is responsible for reading its chosen book, discussing it, and presenting it in some manner to the rest of the class. (Requirement: multiple copies of each book.) Another interest group might be composed of a group of children who want to compile and publish the recipes used in the thematic unit for the entire class.

Task groups are useful for children who need some structure in order to carry through an agreed upon assignment. A place and time for meeting can be specified by the teacher. Care should be taken not to use such a group as a punishment but rather as a help to children who need structure in order to complete a particular activity.

Unlike the other three types of groups, *instructional groups* require a teacher to be present because the purpose is to learn something new or to review a difficult problem. This kind of group, like the others, can vary in size; an instructional group can range from informal meetings of the teacher with a few students having a similar spelling difficulty, to a prearranged larger group needing instruction in using context clues, to the entire class being presented with a new concept in the science unit.

Scheduling

Once school-imposed activity times such as lunch, recess, and gym have been taken into account, the remainder of the school day and week can be scheduled to reflect the children's needs and the teacher's curriculum plans, including those in the thematic unit(s). Daily time should be scheduled for planning, work periods, journal writing, story time, silent reading. Some specific ideas for each of these suggested daily time periods follow.

Planning takes place in the morning with all the students and the teacher making large group, small group, and individual plans for the day. As the year progresses and the children become familiar with the daily and weekly schedule or set activities, the focus during planning time is almost solely on what will be done during work periods.

Work periods should be scheduled for several lengthy periods during the day. During these periods, children become actively engaged in using language as they participate in thematic units and other activities. The work periods can be used by the teacher for whole class presentations, working with prearranged or spontaneously formed groups of children, or with individual children. The bulk of the thematic unit work is done during the work periods.

Journal writing can be done as a whole class activity or at a time determined by individual class members during the day. Journal writing that is begun as the children arrive in the classroom is a quiet and reflective way to begin the day. The teacher can provide a writing model while recording anecdotal notes from the previous day's "kids watching" (see section on evaluation later in this article). First graders who are involved in journal writing from the beginning of the school year use this time to draw and to write or to "pretend" to write. (See Watson's and Crafton's discussions earlier in this volume.) As the year progresses, so will the quality and amount of children's writing.

Story time usually takes place at set times of the day. Activities range from the oral reading of a book by the teacher, librarian, principal, or a parent to sharing of favorite books recently read by the children.

In most classrooms *silent reading* (often referred to as *USSR*) takes place with the whole class participating. However, many children can take the responsibility of deciding when to spend a minimum amount of time during the day in the reading area instead. Others who need more structure can be assigned to a "task group" meeting for such a purpose daily at a set time. It is important that an adult, often the teacher, also be a part of the group so as to provide a model.

Review the day time is the reverse of planning time and often shortens the time necessary for planning the following morning. The time allows children to review and share with their classmates what they have accomplished during the day, particularly during the work periods. The time results in children considering their goals for the following day and provides them and their teacher time for locating useful or necessary materials before the next day's activities begin.

On a weekly basis, it is often useful to set aside specific times for instructional groups in reading, writing, math, etc.. Three specific suggestions follow:

Regular *reading strategy lessons* will be necessary for some or all of the students. Though many of these lessons may be done during work periods, the teacher may find that some lessons will be more effective if scheduled to be done with the entire class or most of the class. The aim during the lessons is to assist children in learning to use strategies such as predicting and confirming more effectively, or to change the students' attitudes and perceptions about reading. For example, the class might have a discussion about the kinds of things they read in the world outside of school, they might share and compare their story endings (see "learning centers" discussion) with a focus on the clues used to construct the endings, or they might participate in a cloze exercise and follow-up discussion to strengthen their use of the syntactic and semantic systems (see Goodman & Burke, 1980, and Crafton, Hill, House, & Kucer, 1980, for reading strategy lessons).

A writing strategy lesson can be scheduled once or twice a week in order to work on one selected writing problem with the entire class. Usually, one child's writing is displayed on the overhead projector for all to see. One problem is dealt with, such as developing specifics to support the child's ideas for finding more interesting ways to communicate the idea, isolating one idea from the composition to be developed further, trying out various ways of organizing the idea, cutting away irrelevant information, or working on strategies for more effective use of a selected writing convention such as spelling (see Murray, 1968, and Crafton et al., 1980, for writing strategy lessons).

Parent letters can be written weekly. The class meets on Friday afternoon during "review of the day" time to review the entire week and to dictate a record of the activity and learning highlights of the week. Each child can copy the group's dictation or the information can be typed and dittoed to be sent home on Monday. The dictation can also become part of a "history" that the class keeps on their year together.

One first grade classroom's daily and weekly schedule is illustrated in Diagram 1.

The Floor Plan

In deciding on the arrangement of classroom space, the main considerations should be to provide work spaces of varying sizes which encourage interaction among children and thus encourage involvement in lessons and activities. Plenty of materials must be available to the children in easy-to-locate places.

Some suggestions for spaces are the following:

The *reading area* should be in a fairly quiet part of the room. Comfortable seating space and plenty of books and other reading materials should be provided. Many of the books should encourage further or repeated reading about thematic unit concepts. For children who are beginning to read, plenty of predictable books like *The Bus Ride* and *The Great Big Enormous Turnip* used in the "Little" unit should also be

Diagram 1

Time	Monday	Tuesday	Wednesday	Thursday	Friday
8:30-8:45 as children arr.	Journal Writing				
8:45-9:10	Planning				
9:10-10:15	Work Period				
10:15-10:30	Recess				
10:30-11:30	Writing Strategy Lesson	Math Lesson	Work Period	Math Lesson	Reading Strategy Lesson
11:30-12:15	Lunch and Recess				
12:15-12:30	Story Time				
12:45-1:45	Work Period				
1:45-2:15	Gym	Music	Gym	Music	Gym
2:15-2:30	Silent Reading				Review of Day/Week
2:30-2:50	Review of the Day				Parent Letters

provided, as well as the literature that has been read to the children during story time. Be sure to provide space for the books that the children themselves write.

The *writing and illustrating area* should provide individuals and groups with places to work on and publish stories and reports. Some individual desks, a large table for writing conferences, and plenty of writing and illustrating materials are required. Though much writing and illustrating is done in the learning centers connected with the thematic units, a separate place for "publishing" allows some space flexibility for such activity and puts a stamp of importance on writing.

A *class meeting area* is necessary not only for morning planning time and review-the-day time but also for whole class or large group presentations by the teacher or speakers, films, and the like. When not in use by large groups, the class meeting area can be used by various individuals or groups who need space for working.

The *listening area* is an important area, particularly for children learning to read. Children can listen to and read along with many of the fine recorded children's stories that are available from many companies. Children can enjoy and quickly learn to read written down song verses as well as highly predictable stories like the "Instant Readers" written and recorded by Bill Martin (1970). Also note that several of the "Little" unit activities were based on recorded stories or songs and may be done in the listening center.

Learning centers should be very flexible spaces. Some may be available for only a day or two while others may be long-term centers. For example, if caterpillars collected in the "Little" unit live to become moths and butterflies, the caterpillar center will exist for a long time. Children's interests can be kept alive by changing resources (books, magazines, filmstrips) available or by expanding the center to include other forms of life, such as tadpoles or ant colonies that will extend the same concept.

Learning centers can be created to encourage children to explore things other than the concepts being taught in thematic units. For example, a way to respond positively to paper airplanes, string tricks, and other "distractions" is to encourage the children involved to write directions and to stock a learning center with the materials necessary for anyone to try the same activities. Such a center may last only a week but will probably require a fair amount of space due to the high interest of the children.

Other learning centers require only a desk or two and may come and go throughout the year. A favorite is the "Finish the Story" center. On Monday, the teacher places in the center a good short story without an ending; the children's responsibility is to read the story and write an ending for it before Friday. On

Friday, the children share and compare their endings and hear the original author's ending. If the story selected was a good one, not a sound will be heard during the reading of the author's ending.

Classrooms like those suggested in this article are often rearranged more frequently than most living rooms in homes. Many of the changes are minor readjustments to supply space for sudden needs or new centers, but occasionally a massive rearrangement is necessary. If so, set up a "Floor Plan Center" and encourage the children who inhabit the classroom to draw up their own plans. Their interest can lead to some purposeful learning of map making and reading, and their plans will contain some great ideas that can be put into effect immediately.

Recruiting Others as Teachers

Many people have many things to offer to your students. Some can even offer them a variety of experiences that the teacher cannot offer. As a teacher, part of your job is to recruit other people who will help the students in your classroom learn. What your students learn will be far richer in the process. And equally important, your students will learn that there are many resources other than the "head" teacher who can be tapped to help them with their learning.

The place to begin recruiting other teachers is within the four walls of the classroom. If there are 30 students in the class, each child has 30 resources plus one, the teacher. Students must learn to ask for and to give help to each other if a classroom based on the ideas presented in this article is to function well. As the year progresses, such a process will become more effective because children will come to know each other well and to understand who can provide effective help in various situations. It is obvious to any of us who have ever taught that the best way to come to understand something better is to try to teach it to someone else. Give all your students plenty of chances to be teachers too!

After you have recruited your own students to teach each other, it is also beneficial to begin thinking about recruiting people from outside the classroom to help the children learn.

Pair up your classroom with a classroom of younger children. Encourage the children in your class to read and write for the children in the other class. Such a situation creates real purposes for reading and writing. It is an ideal situation for older children who are having difficulty reading; it provides them with an acceptable reason for reading and rereading good literature written for the younger age child. In writing, it helps to create a stronger sense of audience in the students who are writing, and it provides a powerful reason for using standard forms in spelling, capitalization, punctuation, and handwriting.

Pair your classroom up with a classroom of older children. Reap the benefits from the other side of the coin—stories written expressly for your children and stories selected and read with the individual child in mind.

Find some parents, grandparents, or children from higher grades who are willing to write down dictated language experience stories and to be regularly available for rereading of the stories. Someone can be scheduled for each work period during the day—even the principal can be scheduled for an hour a week. (This is also an excellent way to utilize a teacher's aide if you are lucky enough to have one.) In a classroom of first graders, the children can keep a folder in their desks of all their completed drawings, ready for the time when a "secretary" is available to write down what the children have to say about the drawings.

During planning time with the children, consider what "experts" or organizations are available as resources for the upcoming or current thematic units. Invitations to the classroom and/or field trips out of the classroom can make these experts available to your students. In this day of small budgets, think about how to handle other than whole class field trips: for example, individuals can make field trips with their parents or a volunteer parent can take a group of students during out-of-school time. Such trips produce real reasons for communicating what was learned to the remainder of the class, either orally or in written form.

Evaluation

Formal tests, though useful for some purposes, do not provide the extent and quality of information available from "kid watching" (Goodman, 1978) on a day-to-day basis. Besides teacher observations, the students' own opinions of their progress as well as student products provide a wealth of information about children's growth, information that can be readily understood by both parents and children. Such information, unlike the information provided in most formal tests, is also extremely useful in instructional decision making.

The problem becomes one of collecting teacher observations, children's products, and children's opinions in a way that is manageable for both students and teachers. Some ideas follow and are intended as additions or alternatives to the suggestions in Ammon's article in this book.

During journal writing time, the teacher can provide a writing model for children by utilizing the time to record anecdotes about individual children and/or about groups that are currently meeting. Begin with a page per child and per group; a loose-leaf notebook affords the addition and reorganization of pages as needed. Periodically share these notes with the students and their parents. The students will begin suggesting things to record that you might have otherwise forgotten (or not considered important). And parents are thrilled to see that their children are being carefully observed.

Keep a folder containing samples of each child's writing; ordinarily children will choose their best pieces. If the piece is to be used for another reason (to go home for sharing, to be included in a class book, for example) make a Xerox copy for the folder. Teachers, parents, and children themselves will be able to see progress in both form and content over time in a very concrete way.

Children's progress in making sense can be charted over time by using the Reading Miscue Inventory Conference Form (Goodman & Burke, pre-publication). Printed index cards should contain the information shown in Diagram 2.

Diagram 2

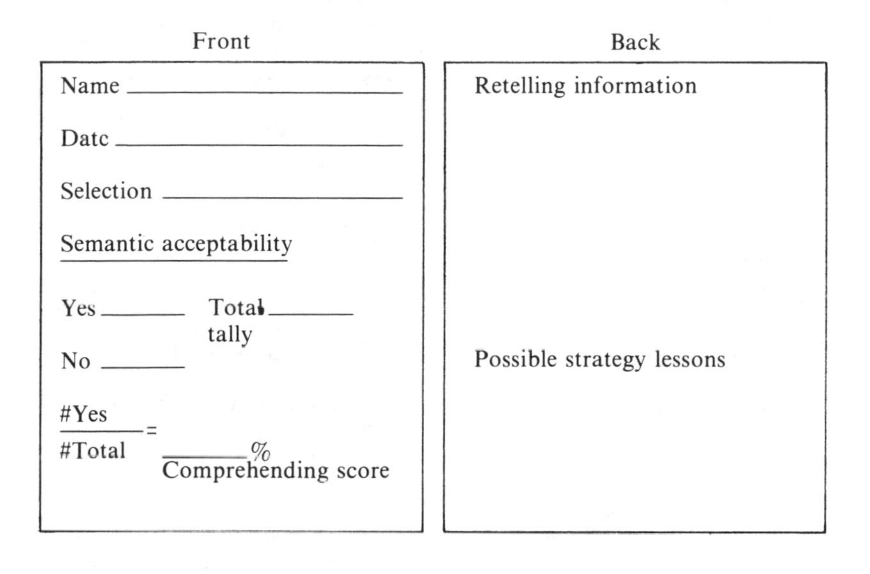

As the child reads orally, a tally should be recorded for each sentence: semantically acceptable (yes) or unacceptable (no). The percentage of semantically acceptable sentences will provide information over a period of time as to how well the child attempts to make sense of texts as s/he reads. Notes should also be made concerning the child's comprehension of the reading and possible strategy lessons. This information is highly useful for decision making concerning both lessons that are necessary for the individual child and for possible instructional groupings.

A record can be kept of the amount and kind of children's reading by the children themselves. Again, index cards can be easily printed and stored. The formats shown in Diagram 3 are suggested by Goodman and Watson (1977).

Diagram 3

For younger children	(reverse side)
Your name ________________ Book title ________________	Did you finish the book? Yes ☐ No ☐ Did you like the book? ☺ 😐 ☹ Yes ☐ Some ☐ No ☐

For older children	(reverse side)
Name ________________ Type of material (book, magazine, newspaper, brochure, my own story, class book) Title ________________	Did you finish the material? ____ If not, why not? ________ Would you recommend the book to anyone else? ________ To whom? (List names) ______ ________________ What would you like to read (about) next? ________ ________________

References

Crafton, Linda K., Hill, Mary W., House, Anitra L., & Kucer, Steven B. Language instruction from theoretical abstraction to classroom application. In R.F. Carey (Ed.), *Occasional papers in language and reading*. Bloomington, Indiana: Indiana University School of Education, 1980.

Goodman, Yetta M. Kid watching: An alternative to testing. *National Elementary Principal*, 1978, *57*, 41-45.

Goodman, Yetta M., & Burke, Carolyn. *Reading strategies: Focus on comprehension*. New York: Holt, Rinehart & Winston, 1980.

Goodman, Yetta M., & Burke, Carolyn. *The reading miscue inventory evaluation form*. University of Arizona and Indiana University.

Goodman, Yetta M., & Watson, Dorothy J. A reading program to live with: Focus on comprehension. *Language Arts*, 1977, *54*, 866-879.

Hutchinson, Janice. A lot can be said about little. Unpublished paper, University of Colorado at Denver, 1980.
Martin, Bill, Jr. *Instant readers.* New York: Holt, Rinehart & Winston, 1970.
Murray, Donald. *A writer teaches writing: A practical method of teaching composition.* Boston: Houghton Mifflin, 1968.
Rhodes, Lynn K. I can read: Predictable books as resources for reading and writing instruction. *Reading Teacher*, 1981, *34*, 511-518.

A Bibliography of "Little" Unit Resources

Barton, Byron. *Buzz, buzz, buzz.* New York: Scholastic, 1973.
Barty, Billy. *The little mouse that roared.* North Hollywood, California: Arrow Records, 1978.
Brown, Marcia. *Stone soup.* New York: Charles Scribner's Sons, 1947.
The bus ride. Glenview, Illinois: Scott, Foresman, 1971.
Channing, Carol. The biggest house in the world. *Frederick.* New York: Caedmon Records, 1976.
Carle, Eric. *The very hungry caterpillar.* Cleveland, Ohio: Collins World, no date.
Ets, Marie Hall. *Elephant in a well.* New York: Viking Press, 1972.
Jordan, Helen J. *How a seed grows.* New York: Crowell, 1960.
Lentil. Weston Woods, 1957. (Book by Robert McCloskey)
Lionni, Leo. *Inch by inch.* New York: Aston-Honor, 1960.
Mayer, Mercer. *If I had. . . .* New York: Dial Press, 1968.
Mosel, Arlene. *Tikki tikki tembo.* New York: Holt, Rinehart & Winston, 1968.
Mousdale, John. *Butterflies.* New York: Wonder Books, 1973.
The popcorn book. Glenview, Illinois: Scott, Foresman, 1971.
Rogers, Fred. Children can, from the album *You are special.* Pittsburgh, Pennsylvania: Small World Enterprises, 1972.
Rogers, Fred. You can never go down the drain, from the album, *You are special.* Pittsburgh, Pennsylvania: Small World Enterprises, 1972.
Selsam, Millicent E. *Seeds and more seeds.* New York: Harper & Row, 1959.
Selsam, Millicent E. *Terry and the caterpillars.* New York: Harper & Row, 1962.
Swimmy. Connecticut Films, 1969. (Book by Leo Lionni)
Tazewell, Charles. *The littlest angel.* New York: Caedmon Records, 1973.
Tolstoy, Alexei. *The great big enormous turnip.* London: Pan Books, 1972.
Yerian, Cameron, & Yerian, Margaret (Eds.). *Fun time weird gardens.* Chicago: Children's Press, 1975.

Literature in the Language Arts Program

Ulrich H. Hardt
Portland State University

Writing in the Commentary column of *Language Arts* journal, Courtney Cazden says: "The most serious problem facing the language arts curriculum today is an imbalance between means and ends—an imbalance between too much attention to drill on the component skills of language and literacy and too little attention to their significant use" (1978, p. 681). Cazden goes on to assert that able and conscientious teachers all over the country in response to real or imagined community pressures are providing endless practice in discrete basic skills, while classrooms where children are integrating those skills with speaking, writing, listening and reading are becoming exceptions.

This kind of skills-and-drills approach frustrates and stunts genuine imaginative growth, even though teachers often rely on literature to help them with the teaching of reading. This emphasis on isolated skills represents an attempt to be efficient: regarding learning to read as a largely mechanical operation, to be taught with the least waste of time by repetition of familiar words, adding new words gradually as facility is gained. The argument for such teaching seems extremely plausible, and has only the flaw that the human mind, which begins as a child's mind, is simply not built that way. Consequently such an approach is not merely anti-intellectual, it is also miserably inefficient, even on its own terms. Emphasis on drills is an emphasis on a "teaching" process in which the teacher is the active agent, the one who knows, and the students are passive, learning through a mechanism of imitation (Hardt, 1981).

Perhaps teachers cannot do away with practice exercises in listening, speaking, grammar, punctuation, spelling, handwriting, and phonics altogether, but now more than ever it is important to stimulate the relationship and integration of those language expressions, not only among themselves but also across the school day and the entire curriculum. And now more than ever it is important to have a comprehensive literature program for all grades. Even though a number of writers have urged planned literature programs for the elementary grades, the school districts that have programs are still in the minority. Charlotte Huck has observed that "All our efforts are directed towards teaching children to read—no one seems to be concerned that they do read or what they read. The means have become an end" (1962, pp. 307-308).

One fairly recent survey showed that 48 percent of the adults in the United States had not read one book during the previous year. Another survey revealed that only 17 percent of Americans had read from a book the previous day, as compared to 55 percent of the British sample. Clearly, we are not a nation of readers, regardless of what we claim our percentage of literacy to be.

Literature in Elementary Reading Programs

Although there are many factors contributing to the small amount of book reading in the United States, one major factor may well be the overemphasis of the instructional or basic reading program to the neglect of a literature program in the elementary school. "Many primary teachers spend over one-half their day teaching the skills of reading, yet never provide a time for children to actually read and enjoy a book!" (Huck, 1977, p. 366). It is indeed the rare case where an elementary school has a well developed vertical literature program that spans all the grades. Many in fact would say that literature is something to be studied in high school, and others would maintain that reading and literature are one and the same, while still others would hold that the literature program is taken care of in the free reading students do on Friday afternoons and during the oral reading the teacher does following recess or lunch. But when we compare that kind of haphazard program planning to the planned approaches in spelling, arithmetic, reading, and social studies, we conclude that we have no literature program at the elementary school.

In the current climate of debate on standards of literacy, there seems to have been a universal scrambling to climb aboard the back-to-basics bandwagon. Nostalgia for an imaginary vanished golden age of literacy coupled with a management model of industrial efficiency applied to the business of reading is in danger of exactly the reverse effect from that intended. Concentration on the skills aspect of the reading process (the *how*) may well leave no time, no resources, and, worst of all, no inclination for concern with the paramount *why* of literacy.

We must substitute Forward to Literacy as the destination of the bandwagon and make it very clear that any satisfactory definition of literacy includes the knowledge and love of literature. All too often in our schools, literature has been merely tolerated and rather patronized as recreational reading with a lower priority than the serious business of information getting. It must be reevaluated as truly re-creational, as the means by which the human spirit is nourished, refreshed, and fostered to its fullest. Its purely recreational function has largely been taken over by film and TV, leaving the re-creational needs of the reader largely unmet.

Some readers may protest that there really is a planned curriculum of literature in the elementary school, since the basic and basal readers are made up mostly of stories and poems. Isn't that teaching literature? No, for while teaching the basic reading skills, the major objective is not to develop enjoyment of the stories and poems as literature. The pieces are selected and used as vehicles for teaching the ability to decode or identify words, to group words within sentences syntactically, to grasp the meaning of the main idea of the sentence and paragraph, and to respond to the sentences in connected discourse. As Pillar argues convincingly in the next chapter, that kind of approach will not foster a love for literature as will her integrated approach.

In high school and college literature classes, students are taught to appreciate literature for its own sake, not to develop basic reading skills. The objective is to help students experience what constitutes a moving poem, a provocative story, a fine play, a stimulating biography. This is not necessarily to say that this objective is more noble than helping with basic reading instructions; it is to say, however, that the two objectives are very different.

One can see this difference most clearly in the primary grades. Generally speaking, instruction in those grades focuses on basic reading skills. The selections in the readers are chosen and taught with that objective. In fact, many selections are written especially for that purpose and others are chosen and rewritten with the same objective; this is why many of the pieces cannot be called literature.

Let us look at word recognition as an example. To make the teaching task manageable, only a controlled number of words is used in a sentence or even in an entire story, and only certain kinds of new words are allowed, words that exemplify the particular linguistic or structural approach being used. So if in a story the author has used a word on literary grounds to achieve emotional impact, rhythm, color, or imagery, that choice can no longer enjoy first priority if the word is to fulfill the skill objective. There it becomes more important whether it is the right word to teach the way a given letter or combination of letters represents a certain word. If the word does not fit the skill objectives, it is replaced by a more suitable substitute. Obviously, not many stories can meet both objectives equally effectively.

The point we have illustrated with the basic reading skill of word recognition we could also show to be true with other reading skills. The more skills a selection is expected to exemplify, the less importance can be placed on literary quality. Teachers and students must not prize the skill of reading as an end in itself, rather it must be seen as the beginning of a lifetime pleasure with books. There are only values derived *from* reading, not values in knowing how to read. A well structured literature program thus becomes an important part of the language arts offerings in the elementary school.

There are many valid reasons why literature should be a part of the language arts program of the child's education.

Children will become readers only if their emotions have been engaged, their imaginations stirred and stretched by what they find on printed pages. One sure way to make this happen is through literature, imaginative literature in particular, where ideally language is used with intensity and power in a direct appeal to the feelings and the imagination (Bettelheim, 1976).

Imaginative literature brings high joy to children in much the same way as sculpture, painting, or music does. Like music, literature brings the stimulation of sound and rhythm. Like painting, it brings the illumination of imagery and design. Like sculpture, literature brings the awareness of space and texture. When it is well conveyed, literature, like all art, leaves a lasting impression. The other language arts have significance in proportion as they relate to a project or problem that the pupil is interested in. But the reading of literature can be an end in itself.

The Values of Literature

At least eight direct values of literature can be identified.

1. First, literature brings to children a world of healthy enjoyment, but it is enjoyment different from the pleasure of taking a circus ride. It is true recreation in the original sense of the word: it re-creates the reader as it actively engages thought and feeling. Literature in this respect can be thought of in part as play, voluntary play in which there is a balance between relaxation and tension. Huizinga (1950) has said that play brings about renewal of vigor for living and a new perspective on reality. Play is self-contained, finding its own rewards in its own performance.

From the beginning we can bring children literature that appeals to their sense of play, from the rhymes, rhythms, and nonsense words of "Hickory Dickory Dock," to the irresistible repetition in *Millions of Cats*, to the simple repetition and dramatization of the "The Crooked Man," to the humor and suspense in the adventures of Ralph in *The Mouse and the Motorcycle*, to the rousing good times in the rabbit civilization of Richard Adams' *Watership Down*—all are at one level invitations to entertainment in the most positive sense of that word. Entertainment is enjoyable; that which is enjoyable is interesting. When a child is interested and experiences pleasure in literature, the appetite is whetted for more literature, and more reading develops the child's reading ability further. If children's literature had no function other than helping students to establish lifetime interests in reading, this value alone would place it close to the apex of curricular offerings.

2. Children gain insight and intellectual stimulation from reading; it satisfies their seeking behavior. Readers can experience that satisfaction by reading the special edition of Rachel Carson's *The Sea Around Us* or Johanna Johnston's biographies of famous women, or they can gain insight into human behavior through *Millions of Cats*, or find out about human conduct and life in the Elizabethan era through Eloise Jarvis McGraw's *Master Cornhill*.

Books for children may not tell why the characters behaved as they did, but the readers are led to think about the causes of behavior. Good writers frame scenes, select details, focus on elements, and reveal subtle meanings while the readers examine human motives and feelings.

3. Literature brings children balanced and new perspectives because good writing will instill a questioning spirit. What was it like to be a child in Paul Revere's time? What problems do children of minorities face? These questions are answered in *The Courage of Sarah Noble* and in *Roll of Thunder, Hear My Cry*. Young readers may be helped in gaining compassion and understanding for the handicapped by reading *Mine for Keeps*, and Robert Frost's poem "Death of a Hired Man" may help to confront the insensitivity that sometimes marks adolescent youth.

Through literature we test life by sharing experiences with many individuals because literature provides an inexhaustible well of human experiences. We feel sympathy and antipathy for persons quite different from ourselves and find more opportunities for choosing among different emotional responses and courses of action than life itself can offer.

In *A Wrinkle in Time*, for example, readers can learn with Meg about the options of courage, integrity, helpfulness, and resistance to temptation as she rescues her father and a young boy. Or in Robert Lipsyte's *The Contender* readers can experience how they would handle rejection, poverty, and intercultural conflicts. Thus, reading literature aids therapeutically in solving personal problems and helps in teaching the problem-solving process while at the same time presents a wide range of options. It helps readers to understand culture patterns of the present and past and helps them to interpret their own needs for security, companionship, love, and success.

In literature we see personalities quite different from our own and become more tolerant. By evaluating different modes of conduct we deepen and extend our consciousness of the richness of life and gain freedom from the restrictions of singularity.

4. The vicarious experiences literature allows can help readers understand themselves. Literature can reveal the significance of readers' emotions and actions in many ways and can contribute to the improvement of attitude and behavior toward people, things, and institutions. A child sharing the companionship of Charlotte and Wilbur in *Charlotte's Web* may sense for the first time the meaning of loneliness and the obligations of friendship, just as adolescents may measure their own loyalties against the relationship of Jim Hawkins and Long John Silver in *Treasure Island.*

Good writing allows readers to experience a character, just as Scout in *To Kill a Mockingbird* finds out what it must be like to walk in Boo's shoes. Literature affords readers an opportunity to participate sympathetically in the viewpoints, problems, and differences of others or transports them to other places and times. So complete can the readers' identification with the character be that they temporarily forget themselves and view the world as the character views it. Readers may feel that they *are* Ishi, the last of his tribe, and actually sense his pain and loneliness. Or they may empathize with Taro as he battles his conscience when he is given too much change in Matsuno's *Taro and the Tofu.*

Literary sources of empathy need not always be characters who embody all the heroic virtues. They can be minor characters or even animals. Through literature a reader may vicariously observe nature, such as the unusual glimpses of an insect in *Moon Moth* by Hutchins, or readers may be inspired to adventures of the spirit through biographies such as Simon's account of Albert Schweitzer, *All Men Are Brothers*, that permit readers to reach out for themselves to understand others. Literature helps children to relive the experiences of others and thus to deepen and broaden their own personal experiences, build their own sense of values, develop empathy, and alter the the world and themselves.

5. Children's books can inspire a love for language and can help to stimulate the students' own writing. Pupils that are exposed to much fine writing will develop an appreciation for many different and acceptable forms of language expression, for a well chosen phrase, for convincing characterization, for descriptions that create vivid word pictures and emotions. Poetry in particular will promote fluency of language usage and familiarize students with new language patterns, strong sensory impressions, and the world of imagery.

The language of children will reflect both the language they hear and the experiences in which they participate; they learn the joy of language and of language play. And books can provide the inspiration for students to write about their own emotions and feelings, because constant exposure to fine writing will be reflected in students' increased skills in their own oral and written expressions, in their ability to think out and organize their own ideas, and in their deepened appreciation of beauty. Wide reading develops and improves children's vocabulary when many opportunities are given to read, listen, and react to good literature. Improved vocabulary leads to improved comprehension.

6. Some literature exists primarily to stimulate flights of fancy, to delight us with the brilliance of its execution. The whimsical nonsense of *Mary Poppins*, the richness of Keats's "The Eve of St. Agnes," the unrelieved suspense of "The Tell-Tale Heart"—these selections offer enjoyment, variety and escape. Readers can find pleasure in the rolling cadences, the rhymes, the deftly turned phrases, the economy of control or the imagery of language and in such subtle ways rejoice in the literary experience.

7. Another major value of wide and varied reading is that it acquaints students with their literary heritage and gives them a

foundation for future literary experience. The best possible study of literature, of course, would be one that did not fragment it or present each piece as a separate entity. That kind of examination too frequently ends only in cruel dissection of a work or endless commentary on some aspects of its content. Students should be allowed to encounter literature as a cumulative study that adds up to more than a list of apparently unconnected poems and stories. The eminent literary critic Northrop Frye has provided such a theory with his delineation of the structured principles of literature (1957).

Children should be allowed to begin their study early because once they have passed the appropriate age for hearing or reading a book, the time is passed forever. No adult can truly go back and begin with *Peter Rabbit* and re-create the effect the book would have had at age five.

8. I conclude with perhaps the most important value—literature as an art form. In this age of mechanized living, children must have the opportunity to obtain the wholesome re—creation and aesthetic satisfaction that comes from exploring the fascinating world of stories and poems. Literature has the ability to heighten an awareness of the beauty all around us and encourages readers to make unique responses inspired by the suggestions of the writer. This is the aesthetic value of literature, when readers join imaginatively with the author to make new artistry (Rosenblatt, 1978). The aesthetic purpose of literature contributes to the overall health of individuals by giving them aesthetic enjoyment and a sense of well-being, meaning, and inspiration.

In the end, of course, the true value of the effects of a literature program for today's elementary children will be seen in the reading habits they develop and keep for ten or twenty or more years.

In addition to the goal of developing permanent interest in reading we need to nurture desirable attitudes in reading selectively. "Our concern should not be simply to develop interest in reading anything and everything," warns Nila Banton Smith in *Reading Instruction for Today's Children* (1963, p. 387). Rather, we should develop discriminating readers, readers who will choose to read those things which will contribute most to their lives informationally, socially, culturally, and spiritually. "The development of interest and taste should proceed hand-in-hand" (p. 387).

One final point should be made regarding the value of the literary work of art. Although literature should not be used for teaching subject matter directly, it may serve well to supplement, extend, and reveal content in various curriculum areas. The subject matter of literature is the subject matter of life, and life's subject matter lies also in the content areas.

The eight values of literature discussed cannot be fulfilled by an instructional reading program or by a Friday afternoon recreational reading period. Instead, we need a comprehensive literature program in every elementary school.

Recommendations

Ten recommendations for a comprehensive literature program in elementary school follow:

1. Teachers, administrators, and librarians must be committed to the value of literature and its worth in students' lives.

2. Teachers, administrators, and librarians must enjoy reading literature themselves and be able to pass that joy and enthusiasm on to students. This is undoubtedly the single most important factor within the school that influences the students' attitudes toward books.

3. Teachers, administrators, and librarians must begin by making more fine books available to all students, recommending buying and home reading lists to families. There should be books of poetry, storybooks, the realistic, the fanciful, classical and contemporary books.[1]

[1]The American Association of School Librarians recommends that all schools having 200 or more students need well organized central libraries and a qualified librarian. The latest survey shows that two-thirds of our elementary schools do not have central libraries, and the ratio of qualified school librarians to students was 1: 4,261.

4. Teachers, administrators, and librarians must create a climate which will encourage wide literature reading by having books available in enticing and convenient displays, by providing time for browsing and sharing of books. Young students like to find some of the familiar old friends in the school situation.

5. Teachers must allow time each day for the reading and discussion of good literature. Ten to twenty minutes twice a day in the primary grades is more effective than the one longer time block older students can handle. Some of this time should be listed as part of "the reading program" for purposes of curriculum allotment times.

6. Teachers, administrators, and librarians must provide for a daily story hour for reading aloud, where various kinds of literature which students might otherwise miss can be introduced. Here books can be read that are beyond the students' reading levels (but within their appreciation and comprehension levels). A reader or story teller with a well chosen story is almost certain of a positive reaction from children.

7. Teachers, administrators, and librarians should use literature to enrich and vitalize the study in the content areas, suggesting relevant biographies, historical fiction, and personal writings. The classroom should reflect the role of books in the curriculum. The day for a single textbook for all students is gone.

8. Inservice classes should be planned to help teachers stay abreast with the 2,000 or more new titles published each year. It should be understood that educators can learn the literature with and from the children; it is not necessary that they have read all the children are reading, as long as they show an interest in doing so.

9. Review and evaluation committees should be set up to assist with selection of books for rooms and school media centers, and some faculty meetings should be devoted to discussions of the place of literature in the curriculum and the development of lifetime readers. The appropriate language arts journals should be part of every school's professional library.

10. Vertical literature programs, i.e., the study of literature in each of the elementary grades, should become an

integral part of the total curriculum, complete with guides, purposes, recommended books, books for reading to children, suggested experiences with literature, and evaluation procedures. Only when a vertical literature program is in place in the elementary schools will the integration of the language arts be possible to the highest degree.

Conclusion

Literature presents a distillation of human experiences; in it we find a significance comparable to that found in life, and it evokes in the reader an emotional response. Myers talks about insight being the indispensable quality of literature, the ability to see others as writers see themselves, from within (1954, p. 337). Scientists and social scientists look on life externally and consider individuals in terms of the group and in relation to measurable values. The literary artist searches for truth internally, viewing the human situation in relation to the individual and through the individual. As Daiches says, literature enables us to explore the recesses of our head and heart with a torch. History allows us only the natural light of day, which does not usually shine into such places, but literature is an exploration of humankind by artificial light, which is better than natural light, because we can direct it where we want it (1948, p. 24). Both ways of looking at life are important; both must be taught to students, but the way of literature is the internal way, and it is in literature and through literature almost exclusively that students learn the humane approach to examining thought and action.

What is the real place of literature in elementary education? Its place is to provide the verbal element in the training of the imagination. The imagination is not a self-indulgent, ornamental, or escapist faculty; it is the constructive power of the mind (Holdaway, 1979). Hence one should not teach reading passively: reading has to be a continuously active and leisurely growth, as all genuine growth is. Teaching reading and all the language arts will produce articulate people, and articulateness is the highest form of freedom that society can give to the individual.

References

American Association of School Librarians. *Standards for school library programs.* Chicago: American Library Association, 1960.

Bettelheim, Bruno. *The uses of enchantment.* London: Thames & Hudson, 1976.

Cazden, Courtney B. Environments for language learning. *Language Arts*, 1978, *55*, 681-682.

Daiches, David. *A study of literature for readers and critics.* Ithaca, New York: Cornell University Press, 1948.

Frye, Northrop. *Anatomy of criticism.* Princeton, New Jersey: Princeton University Press, 1957.

Hardt, Ulrich H. Teaching the language arts: Toward what end? *Oregon English*, 1981, *3*, 3-5.

Holdaway, Don. *The foundations of literacy.* New York: Ashton Scholastic, 1979.

Huck, Charlotte S. Literature as the content of reading. *Theory into Practice*, 1977, *16*, 363-371.

Huck, Charlotte S. Planning the literature program for the elementary school. *Elementary English*, 1962, *39*, 307-313.

Huizinga, Johan. *Homo ludens: A study of the play element in culture.* New York: Roy Publishers, 1950.

Myers, Henry. Literature, science, and democracy. *Pacific Spectator*, 1954, *8*, 333-345.

Rosenblatt, Louise M. *The reader, the text, the poem.* Carbondale, Illinois: Southern Illinois University Press, 1978.

Smith, Nila Banton. *Reading instruction for today's children.* Englewood Cliffs, New Jersey: Prentice-Hall, 1963.

Literature and the Language Arts for Middle Grade Students

Arlene M. Pillar
Fordham University

Findings from the ever-growing number of studies in response to literature indicate, as Purves and Beach (1972) suggested, that books influence readers "emotionally, attitudinally, and intellectually." They show that experiences with literature enhance language performance, vocabulary development, listening, reading and writing skills, and give insight into basic human values. In a discussion of the functioning imagination so crucial to literacy, Holdaway (1979) says that book experiences "develop a wide range of imaginative operations often associated with the deepest satisfactions that are to be experienced with print" (p. 56). His remarkable book, *The Foundations of Literacy*, is essential reading for elementary school teachers who believe in the primacy of literature.

This paper recognizes that books are constructs that fill many purposes and meet many needs. The underlying assumption is that they not be used for skills instruction, although students' skills may grow as a consequence of having read much good literature. Reading with understanding is central to literacy, and students who love to read show their teachers that literacy means more than just getting the words right.

A Response Oriented Curriculum

Research in response emphasizes the interaction between readers and the text. The aesthetic experience as described by

Rosenblatt (1978) in *The Reader, the Text, the Poem* is a dynamic and ever-changing live circuit infused with the unique meanings readers bring to their reading. This means that teachers can expect no single "correct" reading because response is formulated in terms of the predilections and perspectives of readers. The verbal symbols are the basis for unique re-creations of the text by each reader. When we ask students to write or to speak about the moral dilemma besetting Ann Burden in Robert C. O'Brien's *Z for Zachariah*, for example, we can expect diverse responses that are equally valid to the extent that they are not contradicted by any element of the text.

Whatever the area of language arts we choose to extend or enhance through books—listening, speaking, reading, writing—the response will be a personal evocation of text reflecting increasingly complex experiences that bear upon readers' ever-spiraling understanding of literature and life. Such a stance is supported by research. Arthur Applebee's study (1978) of response indicates that the interaction of a particular reader with a particular work "inevitably differs from reader to reader and also changes over time as a given reader's construct system develops and matures" (p. 132). His findings have implications for the products of language arts activity related to literature. This development becomes apparent after the elapse of some time, and teachers who keep folders of work for each of their students readily recognize the growth.

Galda (1980) found that willingness to accept the possibility of multiple realities influenced children's responses to realistic fiction. Those children who were "reality-bound" saw story events and actions which did not conform to their perceptions of the world as wrong or untrue. Those who were able to accept the idea of multiple realities viewed story events as possible, even when they did not conform to their own experience. In addition to the parameters of cognitive development influencing the various forms response may take, Galda found that the reader's personality is a factor. Teachers who really listen to what their students are saying know the truth of this finding.

Iser's gap-filling model (1974) accounts for the existence of wide ranges of literary response. One text holds potential for different realizations, and no reading can exhaust the full potential because readers fill in gaps in their own ways as they read. For both Iser and Rosenblatt there are only personal meanings that result from individual gap filling. Experiential background is an important influence upon response, and it affects the many creative language arts activities teachers use to extend students' reading. This factor will become obvious as the discussion proceeds.

Literature and the Language Arts

The teachers who would use literature solely as a means to skill development are few. As Hardt has argued, books were not conceived for such purpose-filled ends as teaching language. How could we ever ask our students to read Bonnie and Paul Zindel's touching story *A Star for the Latecomer* to locate compound words or figures of speech? When not considered a pleasure-filled end, literature becomes a chore at which most children are unwilling to work.

What is proposed is that literature become a focus of middle grade classroom experiences, some of which may facilitate receptive and expressive language growth; that is, that the richness and joy of literature become the center of literacy teaching. We know that children who read a great deal read more effectively. Further, their total language portfolio is impressive. This focus does not preclude reading for pure pleasure the way Honour did poetry in Robin McKinley's *Beauty*. That factor is a given. The questions are: How can literature promote growth in the language arts without becoming a means to some instructional end? And how can teachers use children's responses to books as a means to help expand their language repertoire and still insure that reading will be a pleasure-filled end?

The practices suggested are guided by sound principles of pedagogy that permit choices and acknowledge individual differences. Teachers need to understand how easily ends become means in classrooms when the concern is the instrumentality of literature as a determiner of language skills. Teachers using the operational definition of literature as process, necessary for this discussion, understand the literature lesson as a valid experience in its own right—the latter being no mere incidental learning (and, perhaps, the more meaningful in the long run). As Holdaway (1979) says, "We agree that the ideal is to have children sufficiently self-motivated and free in their choice of activities to determine for themselves what task they will take up and attempt to accomplish" (p. 13). With such a tenor permeating the classroom, risks for misusing literature are minimized.

Literature and Listening

Attentive listening is an essential part of a planned literature program in an integrated language arts curriculum; Squire (1968), in gleanings from the Dartmouth Seminar Papers, discusses the need for experiencing literature as an oral art. Children extend and enrich their language by listening to stories read aloud or played on cassette recorders.

Research in listening strongly underscores the potential literature has for effecting language growth. In a hallmark study, Cohen (1971) noted that teachers reading aloud to socially disadvantaged children, who had no book experiences at home, positively influenced facility in listening and increased attention span, recognition of new words out of original context, and recall of stretches of verbalization. Strickland (1971), too, provides evidence that students' ability to listen increased when they were read to by teachers who had been provided with special instruction in reading aloud vis-a-vis phrasing, intonation, and so forth. All that most teachers need, however, is familiarity with children's favorite books and brief dress rehearsal before reading them aloud. Everyone enjoys hearing a good story, and children in the middle grades are no exception. They look forward to listening to books and poetry read aloud daily at a specially designated hour.

Some authors are geniuses with words; Natalie Babbitt is a singularly gifted language-user. The rhythm and patterns of her words in the prologue to *Tuck Everlasting* build a vivid image. Babbitt writes:

> The first week of August hangs at the very top of summer, the top of the live-long year, like the highest seat of a Ferris wheel when it pauses in

> its turning. The weeks that come before are only a climb from a balmy spring, and those that follow a drop to the chill of autumn, but the first week of August is motionless, and hot. It is curiously silent, too, with blank white dawns and glaring noons, and sunsets smeared with too much color. Often at night there is lightning, but it quivers all alone. There is no thunder, no relieving rain. These are the strange and breathless days, the dog days, when people are led to do things they are sure to be sorry for after. (p. 1)

Or, in *The Eyes of the Amaryllis*, Babbitt writes:

> When Jenny woke up in the morning, she climbed out of bed and went at once to the window. The beaming sea lay far out, at low tide, much as it had the afternoon before, and it sparkled in the early sunshine, flicking tiny, blinding flashes of light into the air. The horizon, impossibly far away, invited her. The soft breeze invited her. This was a mermaid morning—a morning for sitting on the rocks and combing your long red hair. (p. 47)

Fortunate are the children whose teachers read words such as these to them.

In addition to experiencing literature through the teacher, opportunities need to be provided for listening to peers, and to cassettes and records. Weston Woods has earned a well-deserved reputation for producing quality multimedia materials. In the sound filmstrip "How a Picture Book Is Made," Stephen Kellogg describes a book's development from originating the idea, through writing, rewriting, editing, printing, and binding. The filmstrip does much for fostering an appreciation of literature. Among the many "read-alongs" (cassettes) produced by Listening Library are *The Wind in the Willows*, *The Call of the Wild*, and *Little Women*.

Poetry, often forgotten in the busy activities of the teaching day, can serve to promote effective listening during story hour. Delight in language derives naturally from reading poetry together, for the rhyme and rhythm and the sense and nonsense have power to evoke emotion. David McCord's verse captures mind and ear! "Pickety Fence" ("Five Chants") and "Goose, Moose, and Spruce" are fun to repeat over and over again. The high quality of McCord's works, collected in *One at a Time*, is the reason he was selected first recipient of NCTE's Award for Children's Poetry. We know that children were listening attentively when, at recess, we hear them chanting "Bananas and cream, Bananas and cream, All we could say was, Bananas and cream." or "In a boggy old bog/ by a loggy old log/ sat a froggy old frog."

Another favorite collection for middle grades is Shel Silverstein's *Where the Sidewalk Ends.* Children laugh hysterically when they realize the party guests misunderstand the invitation to throw confetti and they throw spaghetti instead. For students with more mature tastes, on the very fine recording entitled *The English Poets from Chaucer to Yeats*, Richard Burton recites Coleridge's "The Rime of the Ancient Mariner." And Nancy Larrick has selected some special poems for *Bring Me All of Your Dreams*, including memorable works about dreams and dreamers by well-known writers such as Langston Hughes, Walter de la Mare, Carl Sandburg, and Myra Cohn Livingston.

Small groups of students can present a poetry pageant for their classmates' pleasure. These poetry sharing sessions may be tape recorded and kept on file in the listening center of the room. Or, a troubadour troupe of players may be organized to entertain the school with choral reading by traveling from class to class. One gift of imagination is the ability to produce delight, and poetry in the middle grades may serve its cultivation.

Listening is most effective when children know in advance that for which they are to listen. We can ask them to listen and answer questions by recalling details, to retell a story based on what has been heard, to pantomime a poem or story without words, or to predict an event that might happen once the covers are closed. Care needs to be exercised with the tasks set so that they do not become chores. We walk a tight rope because we know that such activities help comprehension grow, yet we know, too, how easily routinely responding to good books becomes an obligatory exercise.

Feltboard stories told by one child to a group of others is pleasurable for all. Older children can select traditional tales from books with few illustrations such as Andrew Lang's *Blue Fairy Book* and prepare them for feltboard telling. They can design pictures to accompany the exciting texts of "The Goose-girl" or "East of the Sun and West of the Moon" and make their presentation to an audience of rapt listeners. The interrelatedness of listening and speaking is obvious in this type of activity.

Hearing language that has become familiar through frequent sharing of good books and poetry is preparation for the time when children will be reading independently. By listening, students develop a feel for language as it is encapsuled in fine literature. Reading aloud to children throughout the elementary and junior high school years creates an active involvement with literature and develops their sense of value for it.

Literature and Speaking

Literature has an effect upon children's oral language in both their acquisition of new words and the enrichment of meaning for words already theirs. Since as much as 95 percent of all communication may be oral, story time holds potential for extending children's speaking skills in natural and delightful ways.

By the middle grades students can engage in quite sophisticated enterprises such as oral discussions, book review panels, public addresses, and creative dramatizations. Response through speaking can richly extend the text in direct proportion to the ingenuity of teachers' ideas.

If they have heard a great many stories during their school years, children will be secure in talking about them since their experiential base provides the support needed for stating the case. It is important for teachers to set aside time that is not hurried for book talking. These contexts provide opportunities for children to discuss their concepts of justice as they relate to literary theme. For example, Ouida Sebestyen's *Far from Home* has a scene in which Salty Yeager and his great-grandmother, Mam, come to terms with the way some people treat the elderly.

> "Are you all right?" he asked, not sure how to start.
> "No," she answered. "I'm not all right. I'm old."
> Her long shadow swung like a pendulum. He thought of the little cogs of her mind moving here, one tooth at a time, through her life.
> "You're not old, Mam. You get around really good."
> "I don't do nothing good anymore." She scratched at a dribble of last

night's supper on her front. "I do everything wrong. It makes me so mad I could walk through a brick wall. I want to keep house and be in on things. What does she think I am? Winter clothes, folded up in here? Add a few mothballs and close the door?" (p. 85)

Students sensitive to injustice and capable of reciprocity in thinking care about Mam's feelings. Participants in book review panel discussions of this fine novel often reveal deeply felt compassion and humanity for the elderly. Similar discussions evolve for Norma Fox Mazer's *A Figure of Speech.*

Oral reporting can be exciting when sparked by a wonderful book. David Kherdian's *The Road from Home* is the biography of his mother, Veron Dumehjian. Set against the terror of the Armenian holocaust, the story begins with the following two excerpts:

> September 16, 1916.—To the Government of Aleppo.
> It was the first communicated to you that the government, by order of the Jemiet, had decided to destroy completely all the Armenians living in Turkey.... An end must be put to their existence, however criminal the measures taken may be, and no regard must be paid to either age or sex nor to conscientious scruples.
>
> Minister of the Interior, Talaat Pasha

> August 22, 1939.—I have given orders to my Death Units to exterminate without mercy or pity men, women, and children belonging to the Polish-speaking race. It is only in this manner that we can acquire the vital territory which we need. After all, who remembers today the extermination of the Armenians?
>
> Adolf Hitler (p. viii)

This moving story took on special meaning for oral reporting by a sixth-grade student who knew of the Jewish holocaust from his parents. We know that there is little to equal a peer recommendation, and *The Road from Home* was never on the library shelf for more than a few hours before another reader, inspired by the oral report, checked it out.

There are many objects that figure prominently in books for children. The more they read, the more they see the role "things" play in the magic that stories create. A Realia Showcase is a way to display a collection of items related to books. Among the treasures that could be part of the stockpile are the following.

A scarf: *Abel's Island* by William Steig (Farrar, 1976)
A cauldron: *The Black Cauldron* by Lloyd Alexander (Holt, 1965)
A staff: *The Walking Stones* by Mollie Hunter (Harper, 1970)
The signs: *The Dark Is Rising* by Susan Cooper (Atheneum, 1973)

Each time children add to the Realia Showcase they are encouraged to speak about their contribution. By the end of the term, the class should have accumulated a great many objects.

When teachers help students become storytellers, they are helping them develop fluency in oral language. The preparation of stories for telling and retelling engages students in varied creative tasks. Whether through dramatics and puppetry, or the flannelboard, tales told by one or more students to others are enhanced if attention is given to pitch, range, and voice quality. It takes practice to be a good storyteller or storyreader, a fact to which anyone who has tried can attest.

Playing roles, acting out favorite scenes, can become engaging activities for middle grade classes. One group of students did an exceptional re-creation of the scripture-reading contest between Lena Sills and Winslow Starnes in Ouida Sebestyen's *Words by Heart.* There is a safe distance that separates an uncomfortable reality when students use puppets to dramatize emotionally charged issues.

Several drawings to illustrate the important episodes in a book can be the focus of a flannelboard sharing. Three seventh-grade girls did such a presentation after reading *Early Disorder* by Rebecca Josephs. Spellbound by Willa Rahv's suffering with anorexia nervosa, they wanted to share the experience with their peers. The flannelboard talk was preceded by some technical discussion of the wasting-away disease that afflicts teenage girls. Their illustrations showed Willa before and after her self-starving. It was dramatic.

Another way to share books orally is through a "talking" mural. Large sheets of craft paper serve as the background for drawings of the main characters. If Sue Ellen Bridgers' *All Together Now* is being considered, the mural might depict Casey and her grandparents, Dwayne Pickens, and Pansy and Hazard. Large holes are cut in the craft paper where heads would be, and students speak through these openings assuming the roles of the characters portrayed. Talking through the mural, players can present the plot and comment upon each other. Students are eager to try on roles and are less reluctant to participate because they are behind the paper screen.

The expansion of oral language is a natural outcome of broad and varied experiences with literature and the many activities that facilitate creative responses. Teachers who recognize this can be vital to cultivating oral expression insofar as they esteem reading aloud and encourage diversity in reader response.

Literature and Reading

Planned recreational reading programs are an effective method for increasing the quantity and quality of voluntary reading. Studying 275 students, Sirota (1971) found that the experimental group, given a special twenty to thirty minute literature experience daily, scored higher than the control group in total books read and selected plus recommended books read. Further, there was improvement in reading achievement.

Studies with a dimension of systematic exposure to stories reveal the value of literature to effective reading programs. Firsthand experience with the literary heritage of the world forms a strong foundation upon which to build increasingly more engaging literary experiences. Children learn to read by reading, and learn to love to read when the purpose of reading—pleasure—is not confused with goals or techniques of instruction.

How many students do you know who become hooked on an author and read all the M.E. Kerr or the Robert Cormier or the Richard Peck books? These children are our most likely candidates for life-long lovers of reading. Once they know how Cormier weaves suspense and intrigue, making hairs stand on end in *I Am the Cheese*, *The Chocolate War*, and *After the First Death*, time cannot move fast enough until "the next one comes out." How exciting to be the teacher of such a reader!

Often reading-lovers are what they are naturally with no help from us. They come to our classes and inspire *us* by sharing books that we might not have had a chance to read ourselves. Just as often, however, reading-lovers can be nurtured by teachers whose enthusiasm for books has been caught. These are the teachers who love books and know how to sell them.

It is easy enough for readers to locate the books of a single author; they go to the shelves and follow the alphabet. But it takes teachers and librarians with a broad view of literature to relate one book to several possible others and, progressing geometrically, to pass this knowledge along. In *A Gathering of Days* Joan Blos refers to students as abecedarians (p. 63). A knowing teacher could suggest that students read the picture book *A Peaceable Kingdom: The Shaker Abecedarius* by Alice and Martin Provensen to enhance the literary experience. Blos' description of baking journey cake could lead to further reading of Ruth Sawyer's *Journey Cake, Ho!* or William Stobbs' *Johnny-Cake* or other variants of the traditional gingerbread boy story. Mention is made in *A Gathering of Days* of the Hessians who served with Burgoyne and shared his defeat. Teachers could ask their students to read Howard Fast's *The Hessian.* Much like Myra Cohn Livingston's concrete poem "Winter Trees" in *O Sliver of Liver*, reading one book leads to another and another. Teachers need to lead readers to related books that heighten and enrich the primary reading experience.

Another reading-related activity, readers theater, intrigues students in the middle grades. The procedure is simple and the rewards of careful teacher planning are great. Each member of a small group reads the same book. A spine-tingling choice is *Inside My Feet: The Story of a Giant* by Richard Kennedy. After reading comes time for "talking it over." Who are the characters? What are they like and how do they sound? A narrator is selected and character roles are assigned. The story is then turned into script dialogue for each character to read; sound effects can also be added. A readers theater presentation of Kennedy's book will require a narrator, the boy, his mother and father, his dog Harley, two rats, and, of course, the giant. For this eerie story the sound effects might include pounding on a door and sliding the bolted latch open.

Script writing may take several sessions and several practice readings. Students will surely include the giant's refrain:

Inside my bones,
Inside my meat,
Inside my heart,
Inside my FEET! (p. 25)

Finally, using only simple props such as a shotgun and a pair of boots, actors *read* the spellbinding scripts they have written with appropriate expression, stepping forward in turn. The production may be shared within the class or school. In any language arts program this is an exciting way to foster growth in reading, speaking, listening, and writing.

Positive changes in reading attitudes and interests result when teachers provide readily available trade books, time for reading and sharing them through engaging activities, and an atmosphere conducive to reading enjoyment. Literature's role is central in instructional programs aimed to make children life-long lovers of reading. Teaching reading with ungraded materials—books of fine quality—demands courageous and energetic teachers. The task is easier today than it ever was in the past because current juvenile booklists present what Templeton, the rat in *Charlotte's Web*, calls " a veritable smorgasbord."

Students need to appreciate that what is so wonderful about reading a book is that once the pages have been turned and the covers closed, they can always be reopened. Reading a book for the second time is somewhat like visiting old friends. The pervading sense of comfort that comes from knowing how it will all turn out is the web that draws us in and keeps us warm. There are few comparable satisfactions in young lives.

Literature and Writing

A wide background of literary experiences expands language and stimulates a love and appreciation for it. Although empirical evidence in written protocols resulting from literary experiences does not unequivocally support the hypothesis that exposure to high quality literature aids in the development of composition, we do know that story structures such as "Once upon a time" and "They lived happily ever after" appear often in children's creative writing (Applebee, 1978).

Literature is a fertile field from which inspiration for writing may be reaped; and creative composition based upon literary study holds high interest for students in the middle grades. It is a pedagogical truism that unless students have something to say, they will have little to write. Good books are thought-provoking and, given the appropriate setting, students will eagerly comment upon them in writing.

The preoccupations students have with human themes and problems are explored in books especially written to appeal to their level of cognitive and affective development. How am I like everyone else? Dare I disturb the universe? Questions such as these are the foci of many books. Holdaway (1979) says "inner awareness of self and human significance generate tremendous energies of expression of every kind. They constitute a powerhouse of motivation and a virtually inexhaustible reservoir of reinforcement or reward" (p. 164). This means that literature is a potent force for enabling students to organize their innermost feelings. Thus the writing children produce derives from their deep concerns and convictions which were positively influenced by their reading experiences.

A good way to start a writing program stemming from reading is to use some of the textless (wordless) picture books published within the past decade. Although many of these books are designed for young "readers," older students can enjoy writing the text for *Bobo's Dream* by Martha Alexander or *Apples* by Nonny Hogrogian. Jacket covers, too, can inspire writing. Some of the most interesting are for the paperback editions of Madeleine L'Engle's Time Trilogy (*A Wrinkle in Time, A Wind in the Door*, and *A Swiftly Tilting Planet*). Also, the five volumes of Lloyd Alexander's *The Prydain Chronicles* have covers to kindle composition.

Reading poetry, with its surprises and word plays, its wonderful sounds and rhythms, can inspire writing poetry. The humorous twists and exaggerations of light verse are the stimuli for students' approximations. Of the many verse forms they find entertaining reading, few compare with the limerick. In *A Lollygag of Limericks*, Myra Cohn Livingston shows her enchantment with such English places as Skittle, Chipping, Needles-on-Stoor, Yately, and Barnby Moor. N. M. Bodecker's *A Person from Britain Whose Head Was the Shape of a Mitten and Other Limericks* introduces readers to "A Maid in Old Lyme" and "A Bride of North Conway." Middle grade writers read these anthologies and spin off their very own limericks.

The more serious poems in *Go with the Poem* by Lillian Moore inspire comparable writing. The section titles are lines from poems; "I'm the Driver and the Wheel" is taken from "Oh the Skateboard" by Lillian Morrison, "What Shall I Do with the Seed?" is from "There Came a Day" by Ted Hughes, and "When a Friend Calls to Me" is from "A Time to Talk" by Robert Frost. All of the poems paint vivid images that students find a challenge to emulate.

Verses to make one's skin prickle are collected in two books by Lee Bennett Hopkins, *A-Haunting We Will Go* and *Monsters, Ghoulies, and Creepy Creatures.* The sounds of the language in these verses make energetic writers want to try comparable stanzas. The books are full of ideas for children to model.

The more experience students have reading, listening to poems, and attempting to re-create parallels, the more able they will be at ferreting out layers of meaning. In *Edna St. Vincent Millay's Poems Selected for Young People*, there are 60 long poems, sonnets, and nature poems for mature students. "The Ballard of the Harp-Weaver" tells of a mother's love for her son. She burns their furniture to keep him from the cold. This poem says a great deal about the meaning of life and devotion. Middle grade writers enjoy collaborating on prose interpretations of ballads and relate them to the popular music of today's troubadours such as Billy Joel or John Denver.

Nothing needs to be said about written book reports other than they have been misused, overused, and abused. In the article "Individualizing Book Reviews" Pillar (1975) proposes an approach to modify the conventional book report. Creative book reporting does not ask readers to recap plot, theme, setting, and so forth (often only to show teachers the book has been read). Instead, students are asked to use what they have read to extend the text. For example, there is a chance to write a letter after reading *A Gathering of Days*. On page 47, Teacher Holt defends himself by letter against the townspeople's accusations. A group of sixth grade students wrote sympathetic letters in Holt's behalf defending his rights.

Often we hear students wishing that a book would never end. Blos' award winner evoked such feelings and a perceptive teacher, grasping the moment, asked some students to write additional entries for Catherine Hall's diary. The task enabled them to become more sensitive to a literary point of view. Afterwards, a few of the girls decided to keep their own diaries—something that had never occurred to them before having read the book.

Literature provides many opportunities for students to write creatively. When teachers have read the books their students have read, they are better prepared to design a learning environment that makes the most of those books. These days, especially the bounty of first-rate publications will surprise teachers and fill them with joy.

Concluding Remarks

A natural, developmental model of reading integrated with the other language arts should require that literature be read aesthetically, not efferently as defined by Rosenblatt (1978). Books are to be enjoyed for what they are; accomplishing some teacher-set task is a secondary consideration. We must work against Holdaway's observation (1979) that " teaching methods and materials in the last generation have tended increasingly to exclude true literature from the literacy undertaking in the interests of controlled vocabulary or phonetic sequences" (p. 17). We need to move the richness and joy of fine literature into the center of literacy teaching. Each time we give children a good book to read, we give them a purpose for learning to read, a forum in which to develop their language repertoire, and an experience with literacy.

Natalie Babbitt's recurrent image of life as a wheel is an appropriate paradigm for what occurs when children experience literature; it is not always possible to tell where this experience starts or will end. The language arts are interdependent and literary experiences influence listening, speaking, reading, and writing. The language we use reflects the language we hear and read. We must not deny children the language of literature.

That reading books may serve as an instrument for developing skills or understandings should not eclipse the crucial role it fulfills as educator of the imagination. As Hardt says elsewhere in this volume, literature enables us to see alternate realities, extending our lives beyond one place and one time. It expands children's knowledge of themselves and the world at the same time it expands the various aspects of the language arts.

For the purpose of this paper, books have been cast in a facilitating role of a pragmatic nature. Still, we know that they satisfy important needs other than those of the cognitive domain. In *Home from Far*, Jean Little writes:

> Usually when Jenny was sent to her room, she felt it was cheating to read. You forgot all about whatever you had done wrong two minutes after you opened a book. (p. 81)

Jenny knows what Emily Dickinson knew when she wrote "There is no frigate like a book/ To take us lands away." Books, the chariots that bear human souls, are a special resource for nurturing affective development as well as growth in the language arts. The caveat, however, is "handle with care."

References

Alexander, Lloyd. *The black cauldron.* New York: Holt, 1965.
Alexander, Lloyd. *The book of three.* New York: Holt, 1964.
Alexander, Lloyd. *The castle of Llyr.* New York: Holt, 1966.
Alexander, Lloyd. *The high king.* New York: Holt, 1968.
Alexander, Lloyd. *Taran wanderer.* New York, Holt, 1967.
Alexander, Martha. *Bobo's dream.* New York: Dial, 1970.
Applebee, Arthur N. *The child's concept of story: Ages two to seventeen.* Chicago: University of Chicago Press, 1978.
Babbitt, Natalie. *The eyes of the amaryllis.* New York: Farrar, Straus and Giroux, 1977.
Babbitt, Natalie. *Tuck everlasting.* New York: Farrar, Straus and Giroux, 1975.
Blos, Joan W. *A gathering of days: A New England girl's journal, 1830-1832.* New York: Scribner's, 1979.
Bodecker, N.M. *A person from Britain whose head was the shape of a mitten and other limericks.* New York: Atheneum, 1980.

Bridgers, Sue Ellen. *All together now*. New York: Knopf, 1979.
Cohen, Dorothy. The effect of a special reading program in literature on the vocabulary and reading achievement of second grade children in special services schools. Unpublished doctoral dissertation, New York University, 1966.
Cormier, Robert. *After the first death*. New York: Pantheon, 1979.
Cormier, Robert. *The chocolate war*. New York: Pantheon, 1974.
Cormier, Robert. *I am the cheese*. New York: Pantheon, 1977.
Fast, Howard. *The Hessian*. Boston: G.K. Hall, 1973.
Galda, S. Lee. Three children reading stories: Response to literature in preadolescents. Unpublished doctoral dissertation, New York University, 1980.
Hogrogian, Nonny. *Apples*. New York: Macmillan, 1972.
Holdaway, Don. *The foundations of literacy*. New York: Ashton Scholastic, 1979.
Hopkins, Lee Bennett. *A haunting we will go*. Chicago: Whitman, 1977.
Hopkins, Lee Bennett. *Monsters, ghoulies, and creepy creatures*. Chicago: Whitman, 1977.
Iser, Wolfgang. *The implied reader*. Baltimore, Maryland: Johns Hopkins University Press, 1974.
Josephs, Rebecca. *Early disorder*. New York: Farrar, Straus, and Giroux, 1980.
Kennedy, Richard. *Inside my feet: The story of a giant*. New York: Harper, 1979.
Kherdian, David. *The road from home: The story of an Armenian girl*. New York: Greenwillow, 1979.
Lang, Andrew (Ed.). *The blue fairy book*. New York: Dover, 1965.
Larrick, Nancy (Selector). *Bring me all of your dreams*. New York: M. Evans, 1980.
L'Engle, Madeleine. *A swiftly tilting planet*. New York: Farrar, Straus and Giroux, 1978.
L'Engle, Madeleine. *A wind in the door*. New York: Farrar, Straus and Giroux, 1973.
L'Engle, Madeleine. *A wrinkle in time*. New York: Farrar, Straus and Giroux, 1962.
Listening Library Productions, Old Greenwich, Connecticut.
Little, Jean. *Home from far*. Boston: Little, Brown, 1965.
Livingston, Myra Cohn. *A lollygag of limericks*. New York: Atheneum, 1978.
Livingston, Myra Cohn. *O sliver of liver*. New York: Atheneum, 1979.
Mazer, Norma Fox. *A figure of speech*. New York: Delacorte, 1973.
McCord, David. *One at a time*. Boston: Little, Brown, 1974.
McKinley, Robin. *Beauty: A retelling of the story of beauty and the beast*. New York: Harper & Row, 1978.
Millay, Edna St. Vincent. *Edna St. Vincent Millay's poems selected for young people*. New York: Harper & Row, 1929.
Moore, Lillian. *Go with the poem*. New York: McGraw-Hill, 1979.
O'Brien, Robert C. *Z for Zachariah*. New York: Atheneum, 1975.
Pillar, Arlene M. Individualizing book reviews. *Elementary English*, 1975, *52*, 467-469.
Provensen, Alice, & Provensen, Martin. *A peaceable kingdom: The shaker abecedarius*. New York: Viking, 1978.
Purves, Alan C., & Beach, Richard. *Literature and the reader: Research in response to literature, reading interests, and the teaching of literature*. Final Report to the National Endowment for the Humanities. Project Number H 69-0-129. Urbana-Champaign, Illinois: University of Illinois, September 1969-January 1972.
Rosenblatt, Louise M. *The reader, the text, the poem*. Carbondale, Illinois: Southern Illinois University Press, 1978.
Samuel Taylor Coleridge from *The English poets from Chaucer to Yeats*. Decca Records.
Sawyer, Ruth. *Journey cake, ho!* New York: Viking, 1953.
Sebestyen, Ouida. *Far from home*. Boston: Little, Brown, 1980.
Sebestyen, Ouida. *Words by heart*. Boston: Little, Brown, 1979.
Silverstein, Shel. *Where the sidewalk ends*. New York: Harper & Row, 1974.
Sirota, Beverly. The effect of a planned literature program of daily oral reading by the teacher on the voluntary reading of fifth grade children. Unpublished doctoral dissertation, New York University, 1971.

Squire, James R. (Ed.). *Response to literature: The Dartmouth seminar papers.* Urbana, Illinois: National Council of Teachers of English, 1968.

Stobbs, William. *Johnny cake.* New York: Viking, 1973.

Strickland, Dorothy. The effects of a special program on the oral language expansion of linguistically different, Negro, kindergarten children. Unpublished doctoral dissertation, New York University, 1971.

Weston Woods Studio, Weston, Connecticut.

Zindel, Bonnie, & Zindel, Paul. *A star for the latecomer.* New York: Harper & Row, 1980.

Organizing the Secondary Classroom for Language Learning: A Practical Approach*

Nancy Wiseman Seminoff
Northern Michigan University

Introduction

Throughout this book and in the professional literature (Henry, 1974; Loban, Ryan & Squire, 1969; Moffett & Wagner, 1976) the importance of integrating the communication processes (reading, writing, speaking, listening) has been established. As Bruner (1965) submits, "The process and the goal of education are one and the same thing. The goal of education is disciplined understanding; that is the process as well" (p. 122). Just as it is more important for students to learn how to learn rather than to learn volumes of information, so it is more important for teachers to have at their command a conceptual framework for integrating the communication processes in the classroom rather than to have detailed plans to employ. It parallels the old adage: you can give a man a fish and he will eat for a day; you can teach a man to fish and he will never go hungry.

The purpose of this paper is to describe one approach which secondary teachers might find useful for involving students in the active process of reading, writing, speaking and listening to explore within thematic units significant topics which are relevant to their lives and a deeper understanding of how eventually to explore such topics on their own. Both knowledge

*Portions of this article appeared in "Smuggling the Language Arts into the Secondary Subject Matter Classroom," by Nancy Seminoff, *Michigan Reading Journal*, 15, No. 2, 49-52.

and strategies are introduced through teacher planning and guidance.

A Thematic Unit

One technique which might be employed as a vehicle for integrating the communication processes into the process of learning is a thematic unit. The unit involves the consideration of numerous reading selections, each selection focusing on some aspect of the same theme. The selections, when contemplated separately and collectively, offer the students an opportunity to gain new or additional insights regarding the idea or theme through a variety of strategies and activities. Coping with a variety of daily problems might be one such theme.

Many junior high school students must cope with an ever-increasing variety of situations. Therefore, a unit on coping provides an excellent opportunity to encourage students to consider these dilemmas and the alternatives. During the initial planning of the unit, consideration should be given to the identification of major concepts to be explored. Next, resources, strategies, and specific activities to develop the concepts should be selected, and the methods for assessment and evaluation of growth identified. Lesson plans should then be designed to provide for the organization and implementation of the components of the unit.

A sample thematic unit on coping is presented in the pages which follow. Specific concepts, resources, and activities are identified. Suggested lesson plans are provided, followed by suggestions for the assessment and evaluation of students' growth/needs.

Unit Concepts

Concepts to consider in a unit on coping include:

1. There are alternatives from which to choose and resources from which to draw in coping with a situation.
2. A variety of influences causes persons to cope with situations as they do.

3. People deal with situations in various ways, and some of those ways are not predictable or apparent.
4. Sometimes it may be necessary to compromise one's position or values temporarily to accomplish a "larger" goal.
5. Some situations appear to lack their original significance when compared to other, perhaps greater problems.
6. A person can gain valuable insights from having to cope with a situation or problem.

Resources

In planning and implementing a thematic unit, the teacher should identify several selections in literature which provide illustrations of how others have coped with a particular problem or situation. These selections, including short stories, poems, or plays, should be identified prior to teaching the unit; however, additional selections may be identified by the teacher or students as a result of exploration during the unit. Other print selections may include essays, quotes, and feature stories. Human and institutional resources may also be identified prior to or during the implementation of the unit. Other media, such as music, art, and film, may be considered as forms of expression for inclusion in this unit.

Literature selections to consider in teaching a unit on coping include:

BOOKS

Beat the Turtle Drum, Constance C. Greene
Flowers of Anger, Lynn Hall
Guy Lenny, Harry Mazer
Head over Wheels, Lee Kingman

FABLES/SHORT STORIES

"A Man Who Had No Eyes," MacKinlay Kantor
"A Secret for Two," Quentin Reynolds
"The Valedictorian," Richard Wright

PLAYS

The Miracle Worker, William Gibson

POEMS

"I Don't Like It," Melanie Scheller
"Lone Dog," Irene McLeod
"The Road Not Taken," Robert Frost
"Your Poem, Man," Edward Lueders

Strategies and Activities

Examples of strategies and activities involving reading, writing, speaking, and/or listening which could be incorporated into this unit are listed below. Although it is apparent that each of the communication processes does not exist in isolation, the strategies and activities are presented here under broad headings—Reading/Writing and Speaking/Listening—in an attempt to provide some organization to these suggestions.

READING/WRITING

1. Book ladder which provides a list of books at various levels of reading or conceptual difficulty.
2. Descriptive writing of feelings caused by specific situations.
3. Guided reading of a selection prior to discussion in small groups or to oral prediction in a class setting.
4. Note-taking from lectures, speakers, or taped commentary.
5. Sustained writing on an assigned or self-selected topic.
6. Uninterrupted sustained silent reading of materials dealing with coping.
7. Writing a children's book which illustrates some aspect of coping with a situation.
8. Writing letters to request information from agencies or institutions which provide specific services related to coping (e.g., social services, mental health clinic, local court system).

9. Writing dialogue to illustrate how misunderstandings arise and how they can be solved.
10. Written questions which provide opportunity for the exploration of meaning(s) in the assigned selections.

SPEAKING/LISTENING

1. Brainstorming and buzz sessions in small groups.
2. Choral reading of poems.
3. Discussions in small groups which focus on the response of individuals to the questions that accompany the assigned reading.
4. Dramatizing excerpts from a selection which illustrates coping (e.g., *The Miracle Worker*).
5. Interviewing resource persons invited to the class.
6. Listening to television or radio advertising to identify propaganda techniques.
7. Panel discussions regarding the ways in which characters in selections dealt with specific situations that required coping.
8. Puppetry to dramatize selected fairy tales or original scripts which reflect a situation requiring coping.
9. Readers' theatre in which selection concerning some aspects of coping is divided into parts to be read orally by individual readers (the voices carry the drama and a minimum of props is required).
10. Role playing to "solve" or consider specific problem situations.
11. Viewing a film (e.g., *Brian's Song*, *The Other Side of the Mountain*) followed by discussion of how individuals coped with the specific situation.
12. Viewing slides, political cartoons, or posters as a catalyst for discussion of the mood (suggested by the scene) or the symbolism employed.

Suggested Lesson Plans

What follows is a sequenced set of lesson plans which incorporates the concepts, resources, strategies and activities listed above. The teacher is encouraged to employ all of the plans to allow for cohesiveness in developing the unit concepts. If the unit needs to be reduced, Plan 7 and/or Plan 8 could be eliminated with the least disruption to the unit's cohesiveness. They are included here to illustrate maximum diversity in the integration of the communication processes within a unit.

Each plan, with the exception of the introduction to the unit (Plan 1) and the culminating activity (Plan 9), is divided into the following subheadings:

Title of the Selection
Synopsis of Selection
Introduction
Procedure
Extension Activities

Most of the lesson plans provide more than one alternative under Extension Activities. The intent in providing alternatives is 1) to suggest various ways for encouraging students to go beyond the strategy presented in the lesson, and 2) to allow the teacher to select alternative(s) which seem appropriate for the students in class.

Plans 1 through 6 are intended to be completed in a regular class period. Plans 7 and 8 could be integrated during a two-week period immediately following the implementation of Plans 1-6. Students should be provided class time to read the assigned novel and to complete the independent or group exploration of the selected topic.

PLAN 1 *Introduction to the Unit*

An introductory activity suggested for this unit is to divide the class into groups of three students to brainstorm various situations with which one might have to cope (e.g., peer pressure to conform, death of a friend or relative, physical handicap, loneliness). One student in each group records all possibilities the group generates. It is important in any type of group to convey to students the purpose of the activity, a time limit, and an expected outcome. Time should be provided for a few moments following the brainstorming to allow the groups to delete, to combine, and to organize responses. These lists should then be shared with the entire class and listed on the board by the teacher or a student.

Next, the small groups can generate ways in which people cope with various situations recorded on the board and list resources available to assist in making decisions or taking action. Half of the small groups may consider *ways* in which people cope (alcoholism, withdrawal, confrontation, theft), and the other half may consider *means* which are available to assist people (counseling, religion, social services). A person other than the original recorder should write down the results of the brainstorming in this round; the composition of the small group remains the same. The resulting information can again be considered by the total class and listed on the board.

Students could then indicate on a 3x5 file card their first, second, and third choices of topics or situations for further exploration. Later (see Plan 7) the teacher could group the students for independent exploration according to student interest.

PLAN 2 "A Secret for Two"

Synopsis

"A Secret for Two" is a moving story of an elderly milkman and a horse who share a secret. At first the secret appears to be that the man is growing old and will be forced to retire. Eventually the reader learns that the man has been blind for many years, but the horse continued to help the man with the milk route—that is their secret.

Introduction

Students could be encouraged to discuss the term *secret*. Specific discussions might focus on its definition, possible reasons for keeping secrets, and consequences (e.g., embarrassment, jealousy, danger) of not keeping a secret.

Procedure

A strategy which combines silent reading and oral discussion to predict and confirm meaning by considering segments of the selection in a sequential pattern is suggested for reading this selection. Specific purposes for using this strategy could be to provide practice in predicting outcomes and confirming those predictions, to provide practice in setting individual purposes for reading, and to generate responses beyond the literal level, the ultimate goal being to process print efficiently for meaning (Goodman, 1973). This prediction strategy should be used with the entire class, allowing individuals the opportunity to read silently each segment of the selection and then to contribute predictions to the class discussion.*

The choice of the selection is a key element for the success in using this prediction strategy with a total class, both in the number of predictions the selection affords and in the appropriateness of its interest level. "A Secret for Two" is well suited for this strategy. The story might be divided into five sections, the divisions coming at points which allow for prediction of what is to follow in the next section. Each section should be placed on a separate transparency, allowing the teacher to control the reading by revealing only a portion of the story. Questions regarding what has been read and what is to follow are posed for each section, i.e., confirming predictions and generating further predictions.

A brief description of the steps to consider in reading "A Secret for Two" is provided below (see Tierney, Readance & Dishner, 1980, for elaboration).

Step 1. Making predictions and setting purposes from sampling the title only.

Step 2. Reading the first segment (1st transparency) to test the predictions for the second section (2nd transparency).

Step 3. Appraising the predictions and purposes (from the 2nd transparency); refining, extending, or rejecting the original purposes and prediction (continue this procedure for each segment).

Step 4. Converging upon understanding(s) suggested in the selection and supported by evidence accumulated through the consideration of information in the selection.

*It should be recognized that efficient readers employ prediction strategies constantly. Using this strategy in a group setting, and considering the responses of several students in the group discussion, can serve as a model and an impetus for encouraging individual prediction and confirmation of that prediction.

Step 5. Extending exploration of meaning beyond the initial reading. Although every group prediction strategy does not necessarily require a follow-up activity, students may want to discuss such aspects of a selection as setting, characterization, or mood.

Extension Activities

Alternative *1*. Students discuss the points in the selection where the author provided clues that Pierre was blind.

Alternative *2*. Students could consider a character analysis of Pierre and Joseph by listing under the appropriate heading those words or phrases that describe each character, drawing from the character's actions, comments, and what others say about the character. A brief discussion of the relationship between the two characters and the reason(s) for the secret could follow.

Alternative *3*. Students could collaborate in pairs or triads to describe the way in which a person they know or have heard about has coped with a physical handicap. Students could also begin generating a list of agencies providing assistance for the handicapped or identify laws for the handicapped which could be considered in Plan 7.

PLAN 3 "A Man Who Had No Eyes"

Synopsis

"A Man Who Had No Eyes" is a story which presents an encounter between a successful businessman and a blind beggar. The blind beggar, indulging in self-pity, describes the explosion which resulted in his blindness, the cause of the blindness blamed on the actions of a fellow worker. The final paragraphs of the selection reveal the truth of the situation and the blindness of the businessman.

Introduction

One activity to establish a background is to divide the class into two groups; students in one group are blindfolded while each of the remaining students is to select a "partner," preferably someone who is not a best friend. In a two-minute period the blindfolded student is to gather as much information as possible about his/her immediate surroundings, receiving directional but not verbal assistance from the partner. The roles could then be reversed and the activity conducted once again. This introduction could be concluded with a brief discussion of the feelings of being blind, perhaps accompanied by the recording of descriptive terms on the board.

The terms *inquisitive*, *unamiable*, and *reminiscence* might be introduced in the context of a sentence and the terms examined by using structural analysis to determine the meaning of the root word and the present form of the word.

Procedure

Prior to introducing this short story, teachers should analyze the content of the selection to identify important understanding(s) they hope the students will discern as a result of having considered the selection (Herber, 1978). It is noted that additional, perhaps equally valid, understandings may be considered as a result of the class discussion.

The students should read the selection silently and be given some specific purpose for doing so, possibly to note several characteristics which describe the man who had no eyes. While the students are reading, the teacher is available to answer questions or to assist students with any difficulties.

One way to enhance students' understanding of the selection is to provide a set of structured questions to accompany the selection. These questions can provide maximum guidance by containing items students might choose for responding to a question rather than requiring students to generate their own responses (Seminoff, 1980). Earle and Sanders (1973) have pointed out that while questions that are structured in this way should not be provided with each selection, questions which provide considerable guidance should be provided periodically to allow the reader to simulate the reading process necessary to gain meaning from print with eventual independence. (See Appendix A for a sample set of questions to accompany this selection).

Once students have responded independently to the questions, they could divide into groups of four to six to compare answers to the written questions. Again, as indicated in the introductory activity, students should be aware of the purpose of the discussion, the time provided, and the expected outcome. The fact that consensus is not expected should be made clear; rather it is the differences in the responses and the reasons for those differences that should be explored (Herber & Nelson, 1975). The language of the selection and the logic for choosing a particular response are a part of the small discussion; in addition, students may feel more willingness and opportunity to participate. During this discussion, the teacher moves freely among the groups to stimulate interaction, pose questions, or provide direction.

Students can then compare responses from the small group discussion in the larger group setting. Individuals who have a particular response or concern may be willing to comment. During the large group discussion students might also be encouraged to generate examples of other persons in recent history who have overcome physical adversity to become successful in some way, e.g., football players, Vietnam veterans.

Extension Activities

Alternative *1*. Each student could write a paragraph describing his/her perception of being blind or having some other handicap.

Alternative *2*. Each student could describe in writing an item in a box using only the sense of touch.

With either Alternative 1 or 2 each student's written selection could be placed in a personal writing folder for future reconsideration and revision. A procedure for revision and editing is described in the section entitled "Assessment and Evaluation" later in this article.

PLAN 4 "The Road Not Taken"

Synopsis

"The Road Not Taken" provides comment on choices or decisions one must make in life and the consequences of making decisions.

Introduction

Students could attempt the completion of a dittoed maze in a given time period. A prize could be offered to those who complete it accurately in the time allowed. This activity could be followed by a brief discussion of the types of decisions one had to make in this activity and reasons for those decisions (e.g., dead ends, side tracking). Comment might also be generated concerning how one feels in situations requiring decision-making, especially under the pressure of a time limit.

Procedure

The students should read silently "The Road Not Taken" and respond independently to questions provided to assist them in gaining meaning from the selection. (See Appendix B for sample set.) Once the students have had an opportunity to respond independently, they could compare responses with someone seated nearby.

Discussion of the responses with the total group could follow. As stated previously, consensus is not expected. Rather, it is the examination of individual differences and the discussion of the reasons for those differences that are encouraged.

Extension Activity

As an extension of the discussion regarding the need constantly to make decisions or choices, on the following day students might be asked to consider one of the two poems listed in Plan 5.

PLAN 5 "I Don't Like It" and "Your Poem, Man"

Synopsis

"I Don't Like It" suggests the grass is always greener elsewhere. "Your Poem, Man" invites a consideration of contrasts, by trying untried circuitry, to gain insight about what is.

Introduction

A brief review of the discussion generated by the reading of and reaction to "The Road Not Taken" could serve as an introduction to the two poems presented in this plan.

Procedure

Students could be divided into two groups, each group assigned one of the two poems. Once each group has read the assigned poem silently, a summary of the poem could be provided for the entire class. Students could be asked to respond to the idea guide as it relates to the poem they considered, while the other group listens to the responses, and the process is reversed. Students from both groups could then be requested to respond to the general statements regarding the poems. (See Appendix C for sample sets.)

Extension Activities

Alternative *1.* Students could write an article from the perspective of a newspaper reporter to describe an event or situation in the community that required a decision and/or change. The reasons for and against the decision could be presented, perhaps attempting to convince the reader of the necessity or lack of necessity for the ultimate decisions.

Alternative *2.* Students could interview someone in the community regarding a change that has occurred or a decision to be made. The present situation could be compared with the original one and the positive and negative aspects presented. Students may want to write fictitious reviews of actual situations in which they were engaged.

PLAN 6 "Lone Dog" and "The Valedictorian"

Synopsis

"Lone Dog" provides comment on attempting to be an individual and the resulting projected image. "The Valedictorian"—an excerpt from *Black Boy*—portrays a situation in which the main character must make a decision to accept the speech of the principal or deliver the speech he himself wrote.

Introduction

The pressure to conform and the possible resulting loneliness are considered in the plan. Conformity and loneliness could be introduced through viewing such slides as a single Mariposa lily, a lone Jeffries pine tree, a deserted alley, an open field; examining a poster of a boy in a deserted street; or discussing the appeal of the viewer of an advertisement for blue jeans or cigarettes. Students could discuss one or more of these situations, including the circumstances which surround that situation, the feelings of a person at the moment of encounter, the description of the setting, or the possible appeal of the situation or setting.

One of the visual aids suggested above could be used as the introductory activity and the other used in the extension activity to promote further discussion of loneliness and the pressure to conform.

Procedure

The teacher should read the poem "Lone Dog" to the students, comment on the imagery, and generate a discussion of the possible meaning(s) suggested by the poem. The students could then read the poem as a choral reading. Students could be assigned to one of three groups, each group reading one stanza aloud once everyone has had an opportunity to read the poem silently.

The teacher could then read "The Valedictorian" to the students. Students could be asked to listen for the purpose of describing the valedictorian. A checklist of possible characteristics to describe the valedictorian could be provided for the students to consider either while listening to the reading or immediately following the listening activity. Students could then share their responses and impressions in a small group and with the entire class during discussion period, referring to the checklist as a basis for the discussion. They could be asked to work in pairs to write a descriptive paragraph of either the valedictorian or the principal.

Extension Activities

Alternative *1*. Students could discuss the slides or posters mentioned but not discussed in the introduction to this lesson. The teacher or a student could list on the board the descriptive words or phrases generated in the discussion. Students could then write a descriptive paragraph regarding their perceptions of one of the situations, i.e., the feeling created by the situation or the visual impression created. The descriptive paragraph could be placed in a personal writing folder to be "polished" at some later time or submitted to the teacher for a response regarding a writing skill that had been or is being introduced (see discussion under "Assessment and Evaluation" for elaboration).

Alternative *2*. Personification could be introduced by having students write from the point of view of the lily, the tree, or perhaps a discarded pop bottle. The experiences of being one of these items could be described.

PLAN 7 *Independent and Group Projects*

Students could further explore a topic concerning some aspect of coping which is of particular interest to them. Consideration should be given to the choices identified initially in the introductory activity of the unit (Plan 1). Examples of specific activities or projects include:

- Conducting research on Langston Hughes, his background and use of language to motivate awareness of and concern for the human condition.
- Developing a set of posters or collages using statements and/or pictures to reflect situations which necessitate coping or situations which portray ways of coping.
- Writing and illustrating a book for children which depicts coping with a specific situation.
- Hosting a guest speaker who would share insights and information about how to cope with a specific problem.
- Identifying and dramatizing a selection or portion of selection or play which reflects how an individual or group coped with a specific problem (e.g., *The Miracle Worker*).
- Compiling a directory and a file of information on resources available to assist a person in coping with specific situations that might be encountered in daily living.
- Reading and comparing in a panel discussion several situations which relate to some aspect of coping.

Time to work on activities as well as for reading and group discussion of the novel should be scheduled (discussed in Plan 9). The teacher also arranges conferences periodically with each student or group of students to monitor progress and to provide assistance. Sharing of the projects could be done as a culminating activity for the entire unit.

Plan 8 *Book Ladder*

Students could be assigned to read one of the four books identified in the book ladder described in this plan. A book ladder (Reid, 1972) usually includes books on a variety of subthemes and provides topics appealing to all students. The books are organized in ascending order of reading difficulty and conceptual development. The books selected for the theme of coping are:

Coping with Family

Guy Lenny The father wants to remarry and suggests the son live with his mother. The mother has remarried and the boy feels rejected and manipulated. (RL: 6.3)

Coping with Friends

Flower of Anger The question of how far a friendship should go when that friend is about to do wrong and wants *you* to help is addressed in this story. (RL: 6.0)

Coping with Handicaps

Head Over Wheels A twin brother is in an automobile accident and is never able to walk again. (RL: 5.5)

Coping with Death

Beat the Turtle Drum The story is about the death of a child and the family's reaction. (RL: 5.0)

These books contain content which is of interest to seventh and eighth grade students. The approximate readability level according to the Dale-Chall readability formula is indicated in parentheses and is less than 7.0 for each book to allow students maximum opportunity to focus on the content of the book rather than to struggle with difficulty presented by the vocabulary or sentence length.

Students should be allowed to select or be assigned one novel to read and be provided class time to read it. The teacher should meet periodically with the group of students who are reading the same novel to discuss a section of it. Questions to guide the students' reading should be provided; the students could then discuss their independent responses during the group meeting with the teacher.

PLAN 9 *Culmination of the Unit*

Once the assigned selections and books have been read and the activities have been completed, the teacher could provide the students with a list of statements which reflect understandings suggested by the reading and identified by the teacher for consideration in the unit. The list should not only contain understandings drawn from the selections considered in the unit, but it should also contain understandings which extend beyond those suggested in the specific selections and allow students to indicate their own understandings. In this way, students are employing both analysis and synthesis in developing concepts. As Henry (1974) states, "In synthesis the pupil is not restoring what he took apart; he is making something not there until he synthesized it" (p. 8). Henry goes on to explain, "Only after he has broken up (separated out, analyzed) each of two or more works is a reader able to bring the two together with meaning. But the purpose of bringing any two literary works together is outside either of the literary works, and the quality of fulfilling that purpose does not exist solely in the works but partly in the person who is to do the synthesis" (p. 9).

Students should be requested to consider the list by first responding independently, then to consider the choice in small group discussion, exploring differences and points of agreement among the group members; finally, students should be encouraged to share the possible insights and conclusions with the entire group. Time should also be scheduled to share the information and insights gained from the individual or group exploration of a topic (described in Plan 7).

Assessment and Evaluation

Assessment and evaluation of students' needs and growth should be conducted throughout the unit. Information can be gathered in a variety of ways and judgments made concerning students' progress. Further, the components of the communication processes which need development can be identified and taught functionally.

Speaking and Listening

During the small group discussion of the responses to written questions which accompany the selections, the teacher can note, either by using a checklist or an anecdotal record, a student's participation in class discussions and completion of the assigned questions. The teacher might consider such factors as the extent of the student's contribution to the discussion, objectivity in responding, willingness to consider divergent points of view, and courtesy toward others. The teacher could establish periodically situations in which students form triads and evaluate each other as speakers and listeners. In this situation one student listens to the discussion of a topic by the other two students and records his/her observations, considering factors such as those listed above, and then shares those observations with the two discussants. Neither of the two procedures described here suggests the need to provide a letter grade for evaluation; rather, the comments become the evaluation source and provide an impetus for further instruction.

Writing

Written drafts that students have placed in their writing folders could be reviewed occasionally by other students. Grouped in triads, each student's selection which is to be revised could be read and commented on by the two other students in the group. In some instances the teacher might want to identify a specific organizational or technical aspect of writing for the student to consider in the assessment; in other instances the students should be allowed to comment on the overall content or the impression conveyed by the draft. These comments could be written or shared verbally within the group.

Periodically students should be asked to select a draft from their personal writing folders to revise and edit prior to sharing it with others. In revising and editing a draft, students should be encouraged to consider the organizational and technical aspects of writing. In some instances, teachers may respond to some identified aspect of writing they have introduced or reviewed, providing comment in the margin, using a checklist of criteria which could be attached to the draft, and/or conferring with students individually.

In some instances when students are asked to revise and edit their writing, the reason for doing so should be clearly indicated to the students. Revision and editing may require several attempts before a student is satisfied with the product, especially if the student understands and accepts the idea that refining his/her writing is an opportunity to develop clarity and interest appeal in a piece of written expression (Elbow, 1973). As Calkins (1979) so aptly states, "Revision is a tribute to the potential in a piece. It is not punishment, but opportunity" (p. 751).

The selection chosen by each student for revision and editing could then be placed in a class anthology for others to enjoy. Another way to share the students' selections would be to have each read orally by a student other than the writer. In this type of sharing the students could note, for example, the choice of words, the inclusion of specific detail, or the particularly clear organization of ideas in the selection. In each instance the experience of sharing the completed selection should be positive for the writer.

Reading

Written questions which accompany the various selections to be read by the students are intended to be instructional rather than to test students' knowledge. As such, it is suggested that these answers not be graded (Fillion, 1981). After students have read several selections, the teacher may want to pose the opportunity for a free-response essay, using a predetermined set of criteria, or provide a set of questions to help determine the extent of a student's ability to read and gain meaning from print. Small group discussions can be used for the same purpose. This information should be used to plan future instruction.

Questions posed to students, whether for instructional purposes or for test purposes, should possess characteristics of effective questions as identified in the professional literature (Riegle, 1975; Seminoff, 1980) for maximum usefulness.

Integration of the Communication Processes

The emphasis throughout this paper is the integration of reading, writing, speaking, and listening for concept development. Using a central focus or theme, instruction is intended to assist the students to consder printed and oral language in such a manner as to seek a number of possible relationships between ideas and to put this evolving set of relationships into a tentative structure. In this way, concepts and the process for continued development and refinement of concepts evolve.

Strategies to develop various components of the communication processes (spelling, using grammar, noting detail in reading, recognizing multiple meanings of words) should be introduced, emphasized, and reviewed as the need and opportunity arise, rather than presented as separate and distinct skills. It is the integration of strategies to develop and employ the components of the four communication processes in a functional manner that is illustrated and encouraged throughout this article and book.

For example, Hardt and Pillar have already argued that a literature selection may provide new information and insight which the student receives through reading and/or listening. The student probes, reacts and discuss potential understandings, using the language of the selection. The discussion causes a need to reconsider tentative understanding, to revise a tentative conclusion, or to reinforce a conclusion. Having considered several sources of information, the student may continue to refine his/her thinking and to seek relationships among ideas through personal editing. Once again, through written expression the student manipulates ideas, probes understanding, revises the thinking as s/he shapes the message. Elsewhere in this volume, Watson and Ammon show that aspects of writing such as spelling, punctuation, and grammar take on importance only as the need arises to refine the written selection for consumption by others. The response of other readers continues the cycle of the integration of the communication processes.

As Aulls, Atwell, Crafton, and Watson point out in earlier chapters, language users communicate meaning through language when there is a need to do so. This implies a purpose for communication. It seems only reasonable then to consider the purpose for communication and the refinement of the processes for doing so *through* the various subject areas identified in the curriculum. We read or listen to gain information and insight concerning some topic within a discipline; we write or speak to share information or clarify some topic or issue within a subject area. Although a thematic unit for English classes is presented here as a vehicle to illustrate the integration of the communication processes, any discipline could have been considered at any grade level. Further, other types of organization could be used. Thus a generic unit or stylistic unit might be equally appropriate in literature; a topical or issues unit may be considered in social studies; or a topical unit may be used in science or mathematics. In social studies, for example, students could listen to two authors' descriptions of Lincoln the politician, compare and contrast the two points of view, gather additional information and impressions from other print sources, and generate their own written description of Lincoln as a politician.

It is through reading and listening that information and insight can be gained initially, and it is through writing and speaking that the information and insight are refined and expanded. This refinement and expansion in turn calls for additional reading and listening. The search for connectedness of ideas requires the use of all of the communication processes at our command, hence the necessity for integration of instruction in reading, writing, speaking, and listening across the curriculum and across grade levels.

Summary

This article has considered both the process and the product in organizing the secondary school classroom for language growth. On the one level the teacher is provided with a conceptual model to consider in interfacing of the communication processes (reading, writing, speaking, listening) for concept development. Specific materials and sample lesson plans are included for illustration purposes for the teachers' consideration. On a second and equally important level, the student is provided with a procedure for integrating the communication processes which are vital to language growth and concept learning. Moffett and Wagner (1976) aptly state:

> We cannot pluck language out and place it under glass.... Wholeness is the key.... The environment for language learning must preserve the truth about language: as the main ingredient in our symbolic life it not only operates within every aspect of our lives but part of its very function is to integrate the diversity of experience into a harmonious whole. Keeping this always in mind makes teaching language far more successful. (pp. 40, 51)

References

Bruner, J.S. *On knowing: Essays for the left hand.* Cambridge, Massachusetts: Harvard University Press, 1962; expanded version, 1979.

Calkins, L.M. Learning to throw away. *Language Arts*, 1979, *56*, 747-752.

Earle, R.A., & Sanders, P.L. Individualizing reading assignments. *Journal of Reading*, 1973, *16*, 550-555.

Elbow, P. *Writing without teachers.* Oxford, England: Oxford University Press, 1973.

Fillion, B. Reading as inquiry: An approach to literature learning. *English Journal*, 1981, *70*, 39-45.

Goodman, K.S. Strategies for increasing comprehension in reading. In H.M. Smith (Ed.), *Improving reading in the intermediate years.* Glenview, Illinois: Scott, Foresman, 1973.

Henry, G.H. *Teaching reading as concept development: Emphasis on affective thinking.* Newark, Delaware: International Reading Association, 1974.

Herber, H.L., & Nelson, J.B. Questioning is not the answer. *Journal of Reading*, 1975, *18*, 512-517.

Herber, H.L. *Teaching reading in the content areas.* Englewood Cliffs, New Jersey: Prentice-Hall, 1978.

Loban, W., Ryan, M., & Squire, J.R. *Teaching language and literature.* New York: Harcourt Brace Jovanovich, 1969.

Moffett, J., & Wagner, B.J. *Student centered language arts and reading, k-13.* Boston: Houghton Mifflin, 1976.

Reid, V. *Reading ladders for human relations.* Urbana, Illinois: National Council of Teachers of English, 1972.

Riegle, R.P. The logical characteristics of classroom questions. *Philosophy of education, 1975: Proceeding of the thirty-first annual meeting of the philosophy of education society.* San Jose, California: San Jose University, 1975.

Seminoff, N.E. Characteristics of written questions in selected American history texts. Unpublished doctoral dissertation, Wayne State University, 1980.

Tierney, R.J., Readence, J.E., & Dishner, E.K. *Reading strategies and practices: Guide for improving instruction.* Boston: Allyn and Bacon, 1980.

APPENDIX A
"The Man Who Had No Eyes"

I. Place the following characteristics under the character to which you feel they most apply. If you feel they apply to both, then place them under both.

successful
well dressed
salesperson
wheedled
dirty
liar

was blind
cautious
annoyed
clung
bitter

thumping his way
eager
handsome figure
Westbury chemical explosion
wants pity

A Beggar *Mr. Parsons*

II. As you note the characteristics listed in question I, place a check beside the following statements you think are most reasonable.

______ 1. Mr. Parsons was a successful self-supporting businessman.
______ 2. The beggar was a bum who made his living off the pity of other people.
______ 3. Mr. Parsons turned out like he did because he was blind.
______ 4. The beggar turned out like he did because he was blind.

III. Which of the following clues could have made you realize that Mr. Parsons was blind?

______ 1. Parsons only hears the sound of the beggar's cane as he approaches.
______ 2. Parsons has a cane of his own.
______ 3. Parsons has memories of windy pools and lush shrubbery.
______ 4. Parsons had struggled beneath handicaps.
______ 5. Parsons felt into his pocket and pressed coins into the beggar's hand.
______ 6. Parsons seemed to have a great interest in the beggar's blindness.

IV. After considering questions I-III, which of the following sentences seem reasonable? Place a check beside the statement(s) to indicate your response(s).

______ 1. People who are handicapped cannot function in everyday life.
______ 2. People who are handicapped always do well because they want to prove something.
______ 3. People do well because they want to—handicapped or not.
______ 4. Other ______________________________

APPENDIX B
"The Road Not Taken"

Questions

1. Which road does the speaker choose?
2. Describe the kind of person the speaker seems to represent by the choice he made.
3. Why does he sigh when he remembers the road he didn't take?
4. Why does he think he'll never be back?
5. Is the decision described here an easy one to make? Explain?
6. List similar decisions you may have to make at some future time.

APPENDIX C
Idea Guide

"I Don't Like It"

______The first stanza could reflect childhood.

______The last stanza could reflect adulthood.

______The poem could be about moving from childhood to adulthood

"Your Poem, Man"

______The poet is talking about comparisons.

______A person should live a routine life, doing the same things over and over.

______Imagination is aroused by seeing some familiar object differently.

______"Man" could refer to all humankind or to an individual

______"Poem" refers to life.

______"It" refers to life.

______Sometimes we want a situation to change, but then we aren't satisfied with the new situation either.

______We may view a situation differently once we are part of it.

Evaluation in the Holistic Reading/Language Arts Curriculum

Richard Ammon
Pennsylvania State University at Middletown

Evaluation in the holistic reading/language arts curriculum is providing feedback to help children improve their communication skills. Such evaluation is concerned with both the process and the product of communication, since effective communication depends upon both the receiver and the sender. The sender must construct a message appropriate for the receiver, but it is the receiver who makes the final judgments as to the effectiveness of the communication.

Before evaluation can take place, the teacher must create an atmosphere in which the children want to communicate something to someone. In such a classroom one would find, as Hardt and Pillar have advocated, children reading many library books and responding to books through art, music, and drama. They would be writing stories and poems, not for the teacher to grade, but to be shared orally or to be placed in books in the school or classroom library. There would be oral reading and story telling; oral and written reports on many subjects would be presented.

Unfortunately, many teachers focus upon "mechanical" accuracy to the exclusion of whole communication. This emphasis often results in an artificial, sterile atmosphere of workbooks and skill sheets—an atmosphere lacking any genuine interchange between the sender and receiver, speaker and listener, reader and writer. Mechanical accuracy, although important, does not ensure effective communication.

The goal of the holistic reading/language arts curriculum, then, is not only the integration of the language arts but also the creation of real, tangible meaningful communication. Besides engendering greater student interest, such "real" outcomes demand attention to mechanical detail. Speaking and writing, reading and listening are usually more effective when such details are addressed. Therefore, real outcomes promote effective communication, for real outcomes bring together the sender and the receiver in a meaningful forum.

Grading

In practice, evaluation is often confused with grading. Evaluation is part of the teaching-learning experience. Grading is not! Children and parents need to know strengths and weaknesses. Grades do not convey such information. When children take music (or swimming or reading) lessons, evaluation is crucial. Pupils need to know what to practice. But rarely does a grade serve any instructional purpose.

Although for some students grades may have some motivational effect, this effect tends to be external rather than internal—for the sake of the grade rather than for the meaningfulness and fulfillment of the work itself.

> Methods and materials that cannot engage students without grades, candy, coercion, or other irrelevant and artificial motivation, do not belong in the schools. It is not idealistic to assume that communication has its own rewards. (Moffett & Wagner, 1976, p. 422)

In fact, grades tend to foster competition among pupils. Although there is nothing wrong with competition, it is acceptable only when children choose to compete—when they understand that they may fail or lose. But when competition is imposed in the form of grades, children have no choice. We may only guess the number of children who refuse to read or write because they have tried their best but failed in their competition for grades.

Teachers should continue to work for the elimination of grades. (The National Council of Teachers of English has a position paper on grading.) Therefore, this chapter will not address itself to the question of how to grade. However, where grading is required, teachers can determine grades from good evaluation.

How to Evaluate

How should the teacher go about evaluating the communications of children? The end products—stories read, written, and told—should be evaluated from a holistic, intuitive perspective. But, you say, that is being subjective. No doubt it is. But it may be argued that such a basis for evaluation is no more subjective and no less scientific than the list of numbers from which grades are derived. Certainly, such evaluation is more meaningful in terms of the feedback provided.

End products may be evaluated intuitively by asking questions such as: Was the story (written by the child) entertaining? Did others want to read it? Did the children enjoy listening to the story read (or told) by a classmate? Or, was the report informative, interesting? In essence, were the children engaging in effective communication through the production of real outcomes?

However, the end product is only half the concern of the teacher as Watson has already convincingly argued. The process for achieving real outcomes—the planning, the attention to mechanics, the struggles with revisions—is equally important. From inception to completion, the teacher assumes several roles: careful observer, facilitator, editor, and evaluator.

The teacher might observe the following:

Tommy needs help in selecting library books.

Six people in one group is too many; make two groups.

Sam needs to be encouraged to make some revisions.

The teacher might serve as facilitator:

Mary, draw a picture of your story first; then write. You'll have more ideas that way.

Amy, what does your character feel?

John, perhaps you want to compare this book with the other one you read on Benjamin Franklin.

The teacher may serve as an editor:

Can you combine those two sentences?

Jeff, you might wish to outline what you want to say.

Sally, find where you need a period in that paragraph. You have a run-on sentence (or a comma splice).

And the teacher may serve as an evaluator:

Christopher is word-calling, not reading.

Sandy needs to hear herself on the tape recorder.

Ruth needs to correct her spelling.

The important feature of teaching and evaluating in the holistic reading/language arts curriculum is that attention to details comes from working with wholes, not the other way around.

> Composition is not the sum of the topic sentences, transition, subordinated sentence structures, and so on. Nor is reading comprehension the sum of vocabulary organizational headings and inferences. (Moffett & Wagner, 1976, p. 408)

Farr (1979b) related a tale about teaching swimming. After teaching a child arm strokes, kicking, and breathing, it would be a callous individual who would throw the child into the water assuming the child could swim. Clearly, teaching language in bits and pieces does not produce whole, meaningful, effective communication. Yet, when outcomes are real, the attention to details must be present (learned) or the void is obvious to all.

Finally, evaluation procedures must be efficient. No teacher can afford being overwhelmed with gathering evaluative material at the expense of teaching. Therefore, an effort has been made to keep the processes of evaluation as simple and manageable as possible.

Evaluation of the Individual Language Arts

In the holistic curriculum the language arts are integrated. That is, there are few occasions for spelling time or a handwriting time because these skills are subsumed under writing. Nevertheless, in order to address evaluation, it is helpful to focus upon certain of the language arts individually.

Writing

Today there is a movement for going "back to the basics." Although sound educators have never lost sight of quality education, in most schools reading and mathematics are emphasized to the exclusion of writing. Moreover, most instruction in English is based upon exercises in texts and workbooks, even though there is strong evidence that grammar drills do not transfer to the process of composing (Graves, 1977, 1978, 1979).

In the holistic curriculum, the purposes of writing are twofold: learn the process and produce the product. The process of writing parallels the way in which authors write. Through teacher and peer conferences, the children choose their own topics, write drafts, review, and rewrite. With the exception of the final copy, messy papers are expected.

As the final copies are completed one by one, these products are shared, either orally or in written form, with anyone who is interested. The written products may be bound into homemade books and placed in the school or classroom library for other children to read. Or, they may be submitted to the classroom, school, or even community newspapers for publication.

Moving about the classroom, the teacher confers with children, asking questions, eliciting ideas, but never forcing them to write about topics of little interest.

> Billy, yesterday you told me about your pet gerbils. Are you interested in writing about them?
>
> Elizabeth, I noticed that you have a skating badge on your jacket. Would you like to share what you know about skating?

Of course, in the holistic curriculum, writing is not always confined to writing creative stories. One child expressed an interest in hydroponics. Consequently, the initial conference focused upon gathering information about the topic.

Once the children have identified their topics and listed some ideas, they are ready to write their first drafts. As the children are writing, the teacher moves about the room, conducting conferences by asking questions, such as:

> Does "nice" mean lovely, considerate, or friendly?

Can you give me an example of this?
What does your dog look like?

As the children are revising their drafts, but before they make the final copy, the teacher continues conferring with the children, helping them to focus upon style, content, and organization as well as mechanics—grammar, spelling, and handwriting. However, all these skills are taught within the context of the child's writing, not in isolation (Calkins, 1980).

Read these two sentences aloud and see if you can tell where the commas should go.
You have people talking. Let me show you how that's done in writing.
You have three sentences beginning with "I like. . . ." Change two of them.
Take a look at your first three paragraphs. What does your reader need to know first?

Record keeping is done simply by having the children maintain writing folders. Many teachers like having the youngsters keep a Can-Do chart on the oak tag folder itself.

Can-Do Chart

Dates	Can Do
9/16	can write one full page
10/2	can use descriptive words
10/11	can use quotation marks

Anytime the teacher and pupil have a conference and decide that there is something that the child can do, it is recorded on this chart. There, teachers, parents, and the children can easily note progress. In addition to serving as a confidence builder, the chart may be used also for accountability. That is, if the children say they can do something, then they may be expected to demonstrate that skill in future writings. For example, if children note they can use quotation marks, then the teacher has the right to expect the children to use them correctly.

The children's drafts and revisions are filed in these folders. Over a few months it is easy to note a child's progress in writing by comparing earlier works with later ones. Such material tells much more about writing progress than smiley faces or grades.

Speaking and Listening

> For many reasons oral language has been slighted in education. Even if teachers sense uneasily that improvement in the spoken word influences learning in other matters, they are puzzled concerning what measures to take, and curriculum guides seldom cope adequately with the problem. Most important of all, oral language is disregarded in evaluation.... Inevitably, instruction shrinks to the boundaries of what is tested: "Give me the power to evaluate, and I will control the curriculum." (Loban, 1969, p. 101)

If one does not wish to accept this maxim, then oral language in the classroom should be meaningful, having some intrinsic value, and must be evaluated. Since test-makers have not been highly successful in developing standardized measures for speaking and listening, it is important to develop sound, informal evaluative techniques that are based upon teacher judgment and pupil performance.

For example, many children come to school with well developed home-rooted languages. Teachers should encourage them to use such colorful speech, and not curb it through constant correction.

On the other hand, good teachers recognize the value of oral language activities, such as mock television news programs that are based upon the news of the children and their neighborhoods. These forums provide excellent opportunities for working on oral language skills such as organization and delivery. Using the tape recorder, the children may record their preparations for their news programs. Then, after listening to the recording, the teacher might say, "Robert, you have said 'you know' several times. See how many you can eliminate." Or, when a child says, "He don't got none," the teacher might ask, "How do you think Dan Rather (CBS News) might say that?"

This necessary attention to detail results from a focus upon the wholeness of the presentation. For example, the teacher might make these comments:

> Mary, by putting your flannel board figures in order, you won't be as likely to lose your place.
>
> Fred, the boy is happy (sad, frightened, etc.). How should your voice sound?

However, teachers should refrain from correcting and evaluating children's language when the discussions are about social studies, science, or other such subjects. That is, the emphasis should be upon the content, not on the expression. If the child feels that he will be criticized for saying something about Columbus, for example, then the natural solution for the child is to say nothing at all.

Through teacher-pupil conferences and the use of the tape recorder, the teacher and child can maintain a profile chart.

As in the case with all evaluation, teacher judgment is paramount. For example, the teacher must determine whether to work with children on certain grammatical constructions. In kindergarten some children may form the past tense of irregular verbs by adding "ed" (rided, bringed); others may reflect local dialects. The teacher must decide whether these forms will become reduced with maturity, or through straightforward instruction, or whether instruction might be spent better on eliciting or organizing ideas.

Listening, like reading, is a task of comprehension. Just as with reading, much so-called teaching of comprehension is really testing for comprehension. That is, children are often asked convergent, single-answer questions that close out discussion,

Speaking Profile Chart

Name ____________________
Grade ____________________
Teacher __________________
Date _____________________
Type of Setting ____
____
Organization ____
____
Delivery ____
____
Other Comments ____
____
Follow Up ____
____

leading nowhere. Comprehension involves all of a person's prior knowledge and experience tempered by the new information. Therefore, open-ended questions that invite children to use all they know encourage children to think:

> The speaker doesn't tell us exactly when this story takes place. When do you think it happened? What did the speaker say that leads you to believe that?
>
> What do you think will happen next? Why do you believe that?

Such questions encourage children to predict, make inferences, recapitulate, and even generate their own questions and hypotheses.

Once again, the tape recorder is an easy to use device for recording speech as well as responses to listening. This is not to say that the tape recorder needs to be used every time there is a discussion. Once every two weeks is probably sufficient to gather evaluation evidence. Then, teachers may choose to make notes of the dialogue onto profile charts.

Reading

I recently asked a young friend, who is a rather prolific reader, what she does during her reading class in school. She told me about workbooks, phonics, and activity sheets. "But what do you read?" I asked.

"Oh, we don't read during reading!" she answered.

This child's remarks raise some serious questions about the purpose of reading instruction. Is the purpose only to learn skill? Or is the purpose to read, to become lifetime readers? One must ask whether the tail is wagging the dog. Are teachers emphasizing skills because skills are easily graded?

Huck (1979, p. 596) stated that "the best kept secret in education is that children learn to read by reading." This statement indicates that reading skills may be learned in conjunction with whatever the child is reading.

If it may be assumed that the basic skills can be taught and learned through reading, what about comprehension? Too often, the evaluation of comprehension degenerates into a quiz show format. Instead, open-ended questions provide children with the opportunities to share their knowledge about books through their perceptions and experiences. The teacher may ask, "Why did you choose this book?" Or, "How do you think the girl (protagonist) would have behaved in this situation?" Such questioning encourages children to express an opinion about the books and helps them develop a self-reliance on their own judgments.

Huck (1979, pp. 723-724) has presented more specific, higher-ordered questions such as, "Why is it helpful to see this character from so many different points of view?" And, "Which of the characters in this book are best developed by the author?"

More advanced readers might enjoy the challenge of questions posed by author Richard Peck (1979, p. 1):

1. What would this story be like if the main character were of the opposite sex?
2. Why is this story set where it is (not what is the setting)?
3. If you were to film this story, what characters would

you eliminate if you couldn't use them all?

4. Would you film this story in black and white or in color?
5. How is the main character different from you?
6. Would this story make a good TV series? Why? Why not?
7. What is the one thing in this story that has happened to you?
8. Reread the first paragraph of Chapter One. What is in it that makes you read on?
9. If you had to design a new cover for this book, what would it look like?
10. What does the title tell you about this book? Does it tell the truth?

Teachers should, however, be cautioned that questions and responses do not teach comprehension. Once the child has read (or heard) a book, comprehension has already occurred (or not occurred). But questions and responses can help children to re-focus, recall, articulate, open insights, or tie together loose ends.

Veatch (1978, pp. 154-207) has advocated the teacher-pupil conference as a forum for evaluation. Essentially, the teacher and child meet for a private conference in which the child shares a favorite book. The teacher checks the child's reading for basic skills and comprehension as well as higher-order thinking, such as making inferences. Then, follow up may be assigned. The results of these conferences are recorded on a reading profile chart similar to the chart shown.

Since the goal of the reading program should be to build lifetime readers, it is important to keep records of the books children have read. A quick glance at the Profile Chart can provide the teacher and future teachers with a great deal of information about the child's reading habits.

However, the teacher and children may wish to keep a record of all the books the children have read, not just those discussed during the conference. These books may be recorded on a Books Read Chart.

Reading Profile Chart

Name ____________________
Grade ____________________
Teacher ____________________
Date ____________________
Word Study Skills ____________________________________

____
Comprehension ____

____
Personal Positive ______________________________________
Comments
Follow Up Work _______________________________________

____
Books Presented
Title ____
Author ____
Illustrator ____

Books Read

Name ____________________
Grade ____________________
Teacher ____________________

____
Title ____
Author ____
Date started _______________ Date completed _____________
Comments ____

____
Title ____
Author ____
Date started _______________ Date completed _____________
Comments ____

____

No record sheet should ever become a basis for competition. In an attempt to motivate children to read, some teachers have made "bookworms" to which a new segment is added for each book read. This gimmick has two pitfalls. First, it is not far into the school year until the race is limited to just a few pupils. By then, the rest of the class is out of the running, and the motivational effect is lost. Second, the pupils vying for the top spot tend to choose books they can read quickly rather than more interesting, longer books. Again, the gimmick fails to elicit the intended response.

Any record of books read should be brief. It should not be so lengthy that it takes the form of punishment for having read. Its purpose is simply to keep a record of the books each child has read throughout the school year.

In addition to a diet of library books, children should be encouraged to respond to literature through art, music, and drama. Presenting puppet shows and creative dramatics, constructing dioramas and models, designing book jackets, and writing letters to the author are just a few of the many responses children can make to their favorite books. Such activities also allow children to demonstrate their knowledge and perceptions.

Records of these activities may be kept on a Response Activities Chart similar to the one shown.

Response Activities Chart

Name ____________________
Grade ____________________
Teacher __________________

Book/s ____________________
Activity ____________________
Date Presented ____________________

Book/s ____________________
Activity ____________________
Date Presented ____________________

In the design of any profile chart, the teacher should use his/her discretion on planning the format so that a minimum of time is spent noting strengths and weaknesses. While the teacher should complete the profile charts, the children should be responsible for maintaining the book and response activity charts. Surely these records provide more feedback than a series of numerical or letter grades.

Teacher Evaluation

Despite the reports in the popular media that today's youth are not learning, the fact is that American education has produced a most literate society (Farr, 1979). All educators, of course, recognize that problems exist. Some of these problems stem from conditions beyond any teacher's control. But many improvements can be made, not by the federal, state, or district mandates, but by teachers in their own classrooms.

The overriding goal of reading/language arts teachers should be to foster lifetime readers and writers. Moving toward this goal demands continual self-examination by the teacher.

Sometimes teachers have generated excuses like, "I'll never try that idea again" or "It might work in theory, but not in practice" or "We need a new curriculum (basal, method, etc.)." Reflective teachers examine their roles in terms of what is there and what can be done about it.

Am I providing the children with some successful reading experiences, regardless of their abilities?

Am I helping children to view reading as a joyful, humanistic process, or do the children perceive reading as a degrading experience?

Am I providing time each day for children to read independently?

Am I reading literature to children every day, regardless of grade level?

Am I providing frequent opportunities for children to share their favorite books?

Am I providing opportunities for children to read orally? (Older children may enjoy reading picture books to primary grade children.)

Am I providing the children with opportunities to write every day?

Do I believe children will learn (and retain) more from engaging in projects than from doing worksheets?

Do I place more emphasis upon the process than upon the product, or the other way around?

Indeed, it takes the secure teacher to come to terms with these and other questions. But teachers must be willing to take risks, to make mistakes. At the same time, they must be reflective, determined to make the necessary changes to yield a successful experience. Naturally, teachers are more capable of such growth when administrators demonstrate confidence in their faculty. Then teachers are free to make meaningful evaluations, relying more upon their own intuitive judgments and less upon the so-called scientific measuring instruments.

When teachers embrace the holistic reading/language arts curriculum and provide children and parents with meaningful feedback to real learning experiences, you can be certain that children will learn—and enjoy doing so.

References

Calkins, Lucy McCormick. Research update. When children want to punctuate: Basic skills belong in context. *Language Arts*, 1980, *57*, 567-573.

Farr, Roger. What's happening in reading: Goodbye Rudolph Flesch. Speech delivered at the Keystone State Reading Association, Philadelphia, November 1979.

Farr, Roger. *The teaching and learning of basic academic skills in schools: A testimony before the Senate Subcommittee on Education, Arts, and Humanities*. New York: Harcourt Brace Jovanovich, 1979.

Graves, Donald. Research update. Language arts textbooks: A writing process evaluation. *Language Arts*, 1977, *54*, 817-823.

Graves, Donald. *Balance the basics: Let them write*. New York: Ford Foundation, 1978.

Graves, Donald. Research update. What children show us about revision. *Language Arts*, 1979, *56*, 312-319.

Huck, Charlotte. *Children's literature in the elementary school*. New York: Holt, Rinehart and Winston, 1979.

Loban, Walter. Oral language and learning. In James Walden (Ed.), *Oral language and reading*. Urbana, Illinois: National Council of Teachers of English, 1969.

Moffett, James, & Wagner, Betty Jane. *Student centered language arts and reading, k-13*. Boston: Houghton Mifflin, 1976.

National Council of Teachers of English. Policy on grading. Urbana, Illinois: NCTE, 1971.

Peck, Richard. Ten questions to ask about a novel. *Assembly on literature for adolescents: Newsletter 5*, 1978, 1-7.

Veatch, Jeannette. *Reading in the elementary school*. New York: John Wiley, 1978.

Summary and Issues

LaVisa Cam Wilson
Auburn University

This monograph presents the views of the contributing authors—all members of the IRA Committee on Reading and Its Relationship to the Other Language Arts. In three years of planning and discussing, the committe found no fast, easy answers for relating reading and other language arts instruction. Rather, members identified needs for concerted efforts in the development of basic theory, curriculum theory, and effective instruction. Innovative programs need to evolve from an interchange between research and classroom practice. Classroom teachers, administrators, curriculum specialists, theorists, researchers, and teacher educators all have unique perspectives to contribute to the process. Thus some divergence can be noticed in the ideas presented in this monograph. This divergence contributes to the ongoing pursuit of theory, research, information, and application, and the reader is encouraged to join in the search.

There were two underlying emphases for this monograph. The first was that reading and the language arts are interrelated; therefore their teaching and learning should be interrelated, as contrasted to the predominant reading/language instruction today, which is based on a Skills model that isolates rather than emphasizes this interrelationship. The second was that by presenting information which helps develop one's thinking from theory to practice, viable options would be made available to those seeking alternatives to the Skills model which is unfortunately still used extensively.

Aulls, Atwell, and Crafton identified foundations and theories which they deemed to be the bases for curriculum development and implementation of instruction. Language was a common element in reading-language arts.

Aulls contrasted models of reading and language and discussed their relationship to instruction. The Skills model, which does not build on the child's natural acquisition of language, is used in reading and language arts. The Reading Skills model is atomistic, enumerating and teaching subskills, while the Language Skills model relies on decomposition.

Aulls identified language as the interdependent system for the Psycholinguistic model, Discourse models, and Comprehension model. The Psycholinguistic Processing model includes an analysis-by-synthesis model of language. Interactive processing builds on one's own language competence, using cues to fit knowledge of language with knowledge of text.

The Discourse models of language emphasize the importance of the interdependence in the text or speech. Exposure to different types of text, the meaning one brings to the text or speech, as well as the interpretation of that text or speech, determine one's understanding. Comprehension models in reading utilize factors such as memory, problem solving, perception, and attention to determine what affects one's understanding of text.

Within the commonality of language as the relational base for the language arts, Atwell presented variances in approaches to instruction. One separatist approach follows the sequence of language development as a basis for organizing instruction. Children develop oral language before they can interpret graphic symbols; therefore sounds are emphasized to build identification of words and text. Reading text is presented before writing text. Another separatist approach emphasizes the integration of the language arts. Each of the language arts is identified as a separate component which can be related-integrated in instruction.

The holistic approach discussed by Atwell "defines language as a process that relates symbolic, syntactic, and semantic information available within a contextual setting." Emphasis is given to one's use of any and all linguistic forms in language settings. One moves among the lingusitic forms in the process of communication.

The sociopsycholinguistic perspective of oral language acquisition was presented by Crafton. The environment of the child presents specific rules for language usage which must be learned along with structural rules of language.

Oral and written language are encountered naturally in the family and community. Children use hypothesis-testing for both oral and written language and discover the predictability of language. They are involved with functions of language, interacting between oral and written modes. At an early age, children begin to respond to, interpret, and read symbols in their environment. They write, using the knowledge and hypotheses they have about producing print. Children's use of the linguistic data pool enables them to negotiate for meaning, to borrow from any language expression to develop increased understanding or skill in other language expressions.

If teacher educators believe the language arts should be integrated in the school classroom, then preservice teachers should be provided with similar experiences. Rietz developed and implemented such an integrated preservice language arts program. Within this quarter block, reading, language arts, literature, and language acquisition were integrated for the student's acquisition of information, involvement with assignments, and work with children.

The interrelationship of reading and writing as two mutually supportive systems was emphasized by Watson. Prewriting and prereading activities occur simultaneously as children develop facility in using language. The functional and social contexts of language provide impetus to learning both writing and reading.

The thematic unit in the elementary school classroom was used by Rhodes to develop a model for effective language learning which is an alternative to isolated language skills classes.

The unit is designed to actively involve children throughout the day in using all types of language expressions, thereby learning language skills in the context of interest and need to communicate.

Hardt emphasized the need for a comprehensive literature program in elementary schools. Responding to the current emphasis on isolated skills, he stressed that the use and integration of language arts skills be encountered in a well planned vertical literature program. Asserting the need for and legitimacy of a planned literature program in the elementary school, Hardt identified direct values of literature for children. Recommendations for the decision makers—teachers, administrators, librarians—were included to assist in implementing a comprehensive literature program into the elementary school curriculum.

Pillar described literature's contributions to integrated language arts for middle graders. The importance of active responses to literature was emphasized with examples which utilized listening, speaking, reading, and writing, not in isolation, but as interactions which extend and expand children's involvement with the literature.

Seminoff designed a thematic unit to illustrate integration of the language arts in the secondary classroom. With "Coping" as the unit theme, she developed daily lesson plans centered around theme-appropriate literature. Examples were given in reading, writing, listening, and speaking experiences which reinforce relationships in the lessons.

Evaluation as a process and a product of communication in the holistic reading/language arts curriculum was discussed by Ammon. The evaluation of both the process and product involves the teacher in the roles of careful observer, facilitator, editor, and evaluator. Distinguishing between evaluation and grading, he emphasized the importance of specific feedback and interaction in evaluation which is an integral part of the teaching-learning process.

In contrast to focus on mechanics in the language arts, Ammon asserted, "The important feature of teaching and evaluation in the holistic reading-language arts curriculum is that attention to details comes from working with wholes, not the other way around." Evaluation is made within meaningful communications situations, for example, writing a story, orally presenting information to classmates, and reading and sharing books.

The articles in this monograph presented ideas about reading-language arts which range from integrative to holistic. There is no one "best" idea or place on this continuum.

The discussions of relationships among reading and the other language arts were based on the premise that there can be a cohesive program. Theories of language and communication can be used to design programs and instructional strategies in classroom practice which are consistent with that theory. Currently few published programs exist which provide integrative or holistic models for teachers.

Skill development occurs in integrated or holistic reading-language arts programs in various sequences and contexts. The authors have presented strategies to teach skills in a manner consistent with theoretical bases for integrated reading-language arts programs. Their ideas provide teachers with alternatives to isolated skills drill which is used so predominantly.

The classroom experiences included in this monograph cannot be merely copied. They can only serve as models to teachers who must have an adequate knowledge base of psycholinguistics and sociolinguistics, as well as teaching/learning processes, in order to implement an effective integrated reading-language arts program which meets the needs of their particular students. Teachers must design and adapt most of their own programs.

The extent of integration possible is affected by the school organization. In classrooms where students remain with the same teachers the whole day, relationships can be emphasized to develop and reinforce language competence. Departmentalization reduces but in no way eliminates the possibilities for relating a variety of meaningful content, contexts, and processes.

Many teachers desire to make changes in their reading-language arts programs. This monograph has presented information which supports an integrative program. However, there is no one way, no "cookbook" program. The responsibility remains with teachers to make selections which fit with their theories, their students' needs, and the demands of their teaching situations.

A PUBLISHING PROGRAM TO SERVE YOUR NEEDS...

The development of professional publications that uniquely meet the current needs and expectations of reading teachers, researchers, librarians, and other educators is a major goal of the International Reading Association. Your brief responses to the questions below will help us plan for the future.

Teaching Reading with the Other Language Arts

Ulrich H. Hardt, Editor

This book came to my attention through

_______ my membership in IRA
_______ my school library
_______ a colleague
_______ my child's interests in reading
_______ other (*please specify:* ____________________)

Chapters which interested me most were

____________________ ____________________

____________________ ____________________

Least helpful portions of the book were

____________________ ____________________

____________________ ____________________

Topics that I wanted to know more about were

____________________ ____________________

____________________ ____________________

My needs would best be served through

_______ interpretations of research
_______ practical suggestions for classroom use
_______ help for parents
_______ other (*please specify:* ____________________)

Use reverse side for additional comments and free samples.

Especially for nonmembers

Fill in this form if you are not presently a member and are interested in more information about the International Reading Association.

Name ______________________ Professional affiliation __________

Address ______________________ ______________________

______________________ Areas of special interest __________

______________________ ______________________

Please send me the following free items:

A Sample IRA journal ______ (Elementary)

______ (Secondary)

______ (Research in reading)

______ (Spanish language)

Check for FREE SAMPLES!

______ Current *IRA Publications Catalog* of titles and prices

______ Sample copy of *Reading '83* IRA's newsletter to members

______ *Studying: A Key to Success...Ways Parents Can Help*

AA

ira

Forward your comments to
IRA PROFESSIONAL PUBLICATIONS
PO Box 8139
Newark, Delaware 19714

Other Books Published By IRA

Book Number	Quantity	Unit Price	Price
733			
951			
936			
531			
957			
		Total Amount Enclosed US$	

Teaching Reading through the Arts edited by John E. Cowen, 1983, 117 pages.
No. 733 Individual Members $5.00 Others $7.00

Reading Comprehension Assessment: A Cognitive Basis by Peter H. Johnston, 1983, 101 pages.
No. 951 Individual Members $4.50 Others $6.50

Computer Applications in Reading, Second Edition by George E. Mason, Jay S. Blanchard, and Danny B. Daniel, 1983, 223 pages.
No. 936 Individual Members $5.50 Others $8.00

Developing Literacy: Young Children's Use of Language edited by Robert Parker and Frances Davis, 1983, 196 pages.
No. 531 Individual Members $7.00 Others $10.00

Como Crear Materiales Para Neo-Lectores by Arturo Ornelas in cooperation with the International Reading Association, Unesco, and the Organization of American States. 1983, 39 pages.
No. 957 Individual Members $4.00 Others $4.00

First Name	Initial	Last
Street Address		
City	State/Province	
Country	Postal Code	
IRA Membership Account Number		AA

Amounts are quoted in terms of U.S. dollars. Equivalent amounts in local currency, based on current rates of exchange, are acceptable.

Method of Payment
☐ Check (payable to IRA)
☐ Master Card US$10.00 minimum
☐ Visa US$10.00 minimum

Credit Card
Expiration Date ____________

Credit Card Account Number

____
(please verify)

Signature ____________________

Return this form to: INTERNATIONAL READING ASSOCIATION
800 Barksdale Road, PO Box 8139, Newark, DE 19714, USA 302-731-1600